Feathers of a Phoenix

A MEMOIR

Brigid Hopkins

First Printing: 2018

ISBN 978-1-387-80100-8
Publisher Brigid Hopkins

All inquiries may be sent to: www.Brigidmhopkins@gmail.com

Cover Art by Medina Karić and Cecilia Li

Dedicated to anyone who may wonder if love
heals, it is never too late to begin.

Ann Marie,

Your friendship is a supportive
gift that I receive with gratitude.

Love,
Brigid

Contents

Introduction

The gift of aging is that it has helped me look back with a new vantage point at each season of my life, acknowledging that each experience was filtered through my own perceptions.

In order to heal and expand beyond the limitations of my story, I felt th calling to share it into the world. The biggest obstacle in the process of writing is being seen. Many of my experiences have been silently walking with me in my life, kept in the dark from shame and embarrassment. Hiding my shame helped me to feel safe, move forward. I am freeing myself from this oppressive belief and releasing the chains that no longer shelter or serve my safety.

Many years were spent defending myself in a world that wasn't of my choosing. My mother was struggling, the grudges I carried kept me "safe" and they also kept me closed from a world that was giving me experience for my growth and evolution.

Throughout the pages are moments that stand out most in my memory—as most of my memories are fragmented throughout my formative years. They were experiences that shaped me or set me up for the next step along my journey. I've done my best to recall the situations with the most accuracy. Some names have been changed in consideration of the persons named, given the circumstances by which they were associated.

My wish for anyone who reads this is: To remember that in life one may be victimized, but being a victim is a choice. I've learned a lot from my early years, and one of the more difficult, yet helpful things I've learned is to take responsibility for my part in my story. To forgive myself, and with time, others, to lead with my heart, letting it open as slowly as it needs. Because a life with a closed heart isn't one that is felt, it's endured. I am here to live.

The Only Child

I used to think how sad that I was an only child
Feeling blue
Unsure of what to do
Who to play with
Who to be like
We are all an only child
Even in a family of four
Most brothers and sisters I adore
Not born of the same blood
Breathing a similar fire
Each born with our own blueprint
Purpose
Some in ribbons of pink
Cloths of blue
Seldom singing the same song of our family
We know our role
Scripture
Printed in our DNA
To help one another evolve
See themselves
It's not about being owned
Fitting in
Or unique
We stay true to what we came here to do
Destabilize
Reenergize
A sleeping nation
Pioneering a new way
A true way
Using our hearts
Not our mega-mind
Nor greed
To steed the health of our world
We are all the "Only child"
The Black Sheep
That knows how to baa and leap
Unafraid of the backlash
We've been on our own since our first day
Knowing our home is the World
The eyes of everyone we meet
We belong
We sing our own song
We are all the Only Child

Chapter One
Thirty Minutes with My Mother

As I watch the machines monitor the last vestige of life that beats within you, I'm tormented by all the unspoken words, the years o anguish that we exchanged. I want so desperately to whisper: *I forgive you. I know you didn't mean to neglect and abuse me when I was a child. I know that you suffer, and so I suffered.* I can't. Instead, I sit, biting my last nail down to the cuticle. Watching and waiting. They gave you morphine at 5:00 P.M., it's now 7 P.M. I hope to be here when you wake. I'd like to share that your grandchildren were here earlier—the picture they drew is there on the table. It's Mother's Day. I laugh on the inside, as I am now a mother. Here we are in usual form, me caring for you, despite what I need or want. I asked the nurse a while ago to bring me dry shampoo. It's my offering to you, my last attempt at kindness. I wish to wash your hair, to feel an ounce of closeness through your red hued strands between my fingers. Why do you have to die like this?

Its agony watching you slowly wither away, you are so frail. I haven't heard your laugh or voice in days. Your skin is loose and yellowed—your bones are more prominent than your lovely brown eyes. I can't see them anymore. You haven't opened them in 24 hours. I am so pissed; at you, and God, and myself. I need more time, time to learn how to forgive you. How to forgive myself. Sadly, that time will come after you've left. So, I sit here with an internal battle, for all the years that we could have developed a loving relationship. Instead, you found solace in the pills, men, and booze. I always came second to the charms of anything or anyone else. I was your solid; you assumed I'd always be there. Until I kicked you out of my life. What was I supposed to do? I couldn't take your narcissism one more day. Not one more! To have the last two years back—maybe we could have built something other than walls of resentment and animosity?

You never knew how to love me. You only knew how to say it. Numerous actions fill in the crater of those opposing forces; effort, communication, and vulnerability. You sure as hell are vulnerable right now! There is no glory in this. It's lousy timing to a lousy history.

The nurse finally arrives and frees me from the depths of my loathing thoughts. She hands me the dry shampoo. She wants to administer more morphine. They are trying to control your pain preemptively. I ask her to wait just a bit longer—that I'd like the chance to speak with you. She gives us 30 minutes. This is what it has come to: 30 minutes with my Mother.

"Mom, can you hear me? It's Brigid. I hope you can hear me. I'd like to wash your hair if that is ok? It's Mother's Day, and I've brought you chocolates, but I don't think you have the appetite. If you could, please squeeze my hand." I hold onto your thin fingers, anxiously awaiting some response. You twitch, I'll take it!

I line you with warm towels that I took from the nurse's station. As I shake the shampoo onto your hair, there is very little hair left. It was once so lush, thick and vibrant. Where has it all gone? Your breath is faint. You feel like a drafty window. I know you are still here in the room, but I am unsure if you will be with your body much longer. I am gentle with my touch. I do not wish for this to feel anything other than tender. With every stroke, I feel the emotions welling inside of me. I am flush in my cheeks and slightly nauseous. Years of resentments are rushing through my blood. The memories are with us. The way we remember them differs of course. The only emotion I allow is sorrow. The rest are inside of me, readying to fly out. I swallow hard and fast, conscious of my touch on your tender scalp. I ask sorrow to be with me, sorrow to lead me through these last few minutes together. As my tears fall, they wash over both of us. There is no room for me to wipe them, so I let them flow. I feel you beginning to stir. I pull my hands back and look down upon you. You are surprised to see me. You ask why I am crying. I tell you that I feel sorrowful about the circumstances.

You ask, "Am I dying?"

At that moment I have to admit it to you, and to me. I take a deep breath in and allow the truth to come forth.

"You are dying. They know it is cancer, but the results aren't conclusive."

You open your eyes ever so slightly; turn your head to make contact with my line of sight.

"Don't worry, Brigid, I am not afraid. I used to be, but I'm not anymore. I love you, Brigid, I am sorry."

What was earlier a steady stream of tears is now a full-on waterfall. There are many words I wish to share, but all I can do is cry. Slobbery, snotty, uncontrollably cries. I lean down and kiss your forehead. You close your eyes, and a tiny smile graces your face.

The nurse returns to administer another dose of morphine. I hurriedly clean up the shampoo and comb your hair. I tell the nurse that I will be leaving soon. She asks me to take the gifts I brought you. I thank her but share that I will be back tomorrow.

At 2:30 A.M. I received the call that you passed away. I knew that I wouldn't collect your gifts, but they no longer mattered to me. The gift of your apology filled me more than the chocolates or placard with your name that I had left. It has been 11 years, and I still vividly recall our last moments together.

I have forgiven you for the years that we did our best. Forgiven the pain of the abuse, neglect, and manipulation I endured. Those experiences shaped my courageous heart. I am mothering three beautiful children in a way I wouldn't have known if it weren't for your mistakes. For many years I felt anger at not being given a road map, like the regular girls received from their healthy upbringing. What I've come to know now is that you left me a treasure map. The gifts are still unfolding. I am proud to have been your daughter. I love you still.

Speeding down the long hallway, with wooden floors and pictures hanging crookedly along the way, I love the clickity-clackity sound of my clogs. Giggling in sheer delight, because I loved how loud they were! The only pair of shoes I cherished. There are happy memories among the rubble. Some that I hold close to my heart like a treasured possession. Having only five pictures of my entire childhood, thanks in part to my cousin Sharon, these filmstrips of the happy times are often cut short. My story isn't unique, but it's mine. I grew up in such a way I didn't believe the world could see me. I felt invisible, alone and abandoned. Throughout these pages, I have discovered to a certain extent the pioneers of the world are born the "only child." It's a trial of polishing to reveal the resiliency a spirit contains.

I was birthed into a family of Irish and Italian roots. My ancestors Martin Moran (great grandfather x3), his wife Brigid Murray Moran (my namesake) left Castlebar, Ireland, for a chance at prosperity. Martin was a blacksmith, and had leads on employment in Cleveland. The warrior-spirited Brigid Moran left her homeland while pregnant to travel by boat on a whisper of hope. She birthed my second great grandmother Mary on the boat to the Americas. Brigid was given the name "Little Grandma", her stature small, her courage exceptional!

Faith often referred to our earlier ancestors as Shanty Irish. I thought it was because they lived along the canal in a small shanty, like ice fisherman use on the lake to fish. I later learned the meaning of the term (*one who is low class, poor character*) and found it disgraceful given what our ancestors overcame to begin a life here. To travel so far as a young couple, move across the Atlantic and put down roots was brave.

I was born two months prematurely, weighing a whopping 9 lbs. 8 oz.! I must have been eager to come into the world and couldn't wait another minute. The woman who was brave enough to birth me was a fiery redhead named Faith. My mother Mary Faith Corrigan (née Boccia), decided to go to term with me, knowing that most likely it would be only the two of us facing the big world alone, together. I was her salvation; she, my persecutor. I will never know what it felt like for her during those times. All that I have are my own perceptions, demons, and memories of my childhood. From this one perspective, I can try to put myself in her shoes.

She was a single mother with a physical handicap. To my knowledge, no one in our family was on her side cheering for her to have a child out of wedlock. In my family, there were rules to adhere to; all in the name of "looking the part." The story goes that we were once a prominent family in the city of Cleveland, Ohio. My great-grandmother May Tuma owned and operated The Arcadian Recreation on Euclid Avenue, and The Charm House. My understanding is that The Arcadian was a luncheonette; The Charm House was a restaurant and pool hall. May made the family's wealth by also running a speakeasy, though this is unconfirmed. The estate was left in the hands of my great grandmother, Geraldine (Bobo) and Faith. There are questions I wish I had asked; it never occurred to me to look backward in our history. The family had privilege, cars, a large home in West Park, a housekeeper, a driver and, private education, by most standards, a nice life...although most of this was enjoyed prior to my birth.

Two months before I was born, my great-grandmother, May, passed away. She was the matriarch that kept everything together. From the scraps of information I have gathered through stories, neither were prepared to handle the level of responsibility that came with managing an estate. Both my grandmother and mother had deep wounds that they filled in with alcohol, men, and drama. My mother's drug of choice was any type of upper, sometimes amphetamine.

I came down the canal in shame—conceived in shame, born in shame, held by shame.

I didn't know this at the time, you see. I was a bright-eyed, happy to be here baby, ready to give all my love to the world. Most of my early life was lived being left alone, living in rundown apartments, hotel rooms, and guest bedrooms of people I barely knew. We were always on the move, as securing permanent housing was difficult for Faith. She was used to living the high life, now she was trying to achieve that same level of grandeur on a more modest income. The wealth she once knew died along with her grandmother. It was time to be responsible in the world of adulthood. I imagine the pressures were great, trying to raise me on her own, with little support. My grandmother didn't approve of her having a bastard child. That terminology may seem harsh, but that is exactly how I was viewed. The relationship between the two of them was strained. My mother was raised by nannies, often treated as a casualty to a woman who was far too busy to tend to Faith's basic needs. This is my affectation, solely to help me make sense of her neglectful manner.

Faith had a brother: Tony. Uncle Tony was quite the character! He was a six-foot-tall, husky Italian, with shiny black hair and a lazy left eye. He had a gift for storytelling—come to think of it, they both did. Faith, too, was an amazing storyteller. Each time Uncle T. spoke, I was enraptured. I never knew that working as a construction worker in the 80's was such an exciting occupation!   The stories in the family speak of how Uncle T. gave my Grandmother Bobo a run for her money. The reputation he had growing up was as a brute, often looking for a fight with anyone who would oblige him. I knew him as a bullheaded construction worker who was soft and sweet in my company. He was always full of stories from the job and how he almost "broke this guy's face and those guys'." He didn't like it when people disobeyed his authority and would snort just like a bull when he was ready to lose his temper. Uncle Tony was the male role model in my life who told me I was safe, pretty, and mattered. He would tell me often that I was the apple of his eye. Even hours before his death, those were the last words he spoke to me. Oh, and *capiche*, which means *understand.*

I can see them all now; my grandmother in the kitchen with her mother, May--Faith and Uncle Tony running around the kitchen making a ruckus, and my grandmother shooing them out, the nanny swooping them up to another room. Faith felt inferior to Tony's strength. She was born with a handicap to her right arm. When she was being born, she was stuck in the canal, and the instrument used to pull her out damaged her it. They found that it was broken, and as she grew, they put it in a cast. The problem was that they used too small of a cast and it stunted the growth of her arm. It looked odd, but not gruesome. She did have limited use of her fingers for most of her life, until the accident in Lakewood.

For a brief moment in time, I was a newspaper delivery girl. I detested the work but did it to help us make ends meet. We were living in a three-bedroom apartment in Lakewood. It was a decent sized place, not well maintained, but the landlord was charitable about us missing rent now and again. This was the first place we lived for a long stint, and by that I mean four years in the same residence, which felt like a lifetime! On my route that day I took a shortcut to come home and refill my bag. As I approached I was met by an ambulance, police officers, and lots of spectators. I knew immediately that something had happened to Faith. A I rushed through the door, I couldn't see much through the commotion. went back outside and ran to the back of the apartment. When I peered i through the back window I saw her, buried underneath our cabinets! The entire cabinet system had detached from the wall and landed mostly on top of her. That is when she fully lost the use of her already deformed arm and hand.

Luckily, she wasn't terribly injured and we received a handsome settlement from the landlord. While it didn't improve our status, it did, however, keep the utilities running smoothly for a while.

We walked into the YMCA. It was my first time. I was overwhelmed by all the lights, and the size of the pool! Surely, Faith had lost her mind thinking that I would take one step into this pool. I didn't know how to swim, and barely enjoyed taking baths.

My Aunt Mary would always draw a bath for me when I visited her, and I was uncertain of how to tell her that baths scared me. I often felt uneasy being surrounded by water, even if I knew that I could stand up. It wasn't relaxing, as some people find it, instead it created a host of anxious thoughts and imaginative stories.

This pool was so big. Every breath filled with a stingy, medicinal smell. The air hung thick and heavy with humidity and half of the shallow end was filled with people happily splashing around. I wasn't one of those people; this wasn't my idea of fun! I grabbed onto Faith's hand, looking intently at her with the eyes of: I don't know what you have planned, but it's not ok. I do not consent to this!

The next thing I know there is a tall, chipper young man standing before us. He is my instructor and he is so excited to have me in class. He is eager to get started. I dig in harder to Father's hand, she loosens her grip, and I tighten mine.

"Please mom, please don't make me do this. I am scared. I don't want to. Please mom, please no!"

She looks at me with a disengaged smile.

"You'll be fine Brigid, your instructor is well trained, he knows how to help you get over this fear."

The instructor reaches for my hand. I want to tear it off. I am boiling with a fitful rage inside of me. *Why won't she hear my voice? Why don't my feelings matter? This isn't helpful!* I am terrified. I don't care about his qualifications, his smile or his eagerness. I want Faith to take me home and tell me that she was kidding, that this is all a big joke.

She pulls away from me and he reaches down to grab onto my upper arm. I begin to cry, squirm and wiggle my way out of this. I am fully resistant to his efforts of "calming" me down. I don't need to be calmed. I need to get the hell out of here, NOW!

Slowly the rest of the class trickles in and I am the only one in distress. Maybe I am in the wrong class. This can't be the first one. Why isn't anyone else afraid? The instructor begins talking to us about the agenda for the night. We will begin in the deep end with floaties. To help us get more comfortable with certain paddling movements. I am doing my best to swallow this fear, to hide my shame of being afraid. I swallow hard, the hardest I've ever swallowed. I square my shoulders and tell myself *I can paddle in the deep end, I can paddle in the deep end.* I feel slightly dizzy and woozy. I sit down. The floor is cold, damp and comforting. It feels like a new world down here in the murky coldness. I wonder how many droplets on the floor came from my tears. I let my body grab onto the cool tiles and listen intently to his instructions. One by one they put on their vests. He brings one to me and shows me how to adjust it to assure I am securely fastened and comfortable.

The floor is more comforting than Faith or the instructor. The floor is doing its one job very well: holding ground for people's feet. I needed to feel the ground beneath me, knowing that soon they will be dangling with dead space beneath them. Gulp, that's a horrifying thought. A surge of fear races through me again.

Why do people find swimming important? I can't imagine being swept away by Lake Erie, we live too far inland. Any other exposure to water i at will and I do not will it. He walks over to me and invites me to my fee in a low, gentle voice he is assuring me that he will be right there beside me every step of the way.

He walks me over to the edge of the deep end and asks me to jump in. grip my toes tightly onto the lip and shudder at his request. *Whaaat, what did you say?*

"Just plop yourself in, Brigid. It's a little jump, you won't go under. On you take the leap I will follow behind you and promise to keep you upright and secure. Your vest will keep you above the water as well."

I frantically look around for Faith. *Where is she? Where is my mother?!* I see her on the other side of the glass looking in. Her face shows an eager excitement. A look of *go, go, go, just jump in.*

I look up at my instructor; he is looking at me with a big smile. "You car do this Brigid, take a step forward and fall in."

The rest of the class is in the water with another instructor that I didn't meet. They are all bobbing around as they keep paddling. I take one look at Faith and take the step forward. Splash!

Oh no, oh no, what did I do?! I begin kicking my feet and rolling around on the surface of the water. I am in full panic mode. I am flailing, flopping, and kicking screaming. I can't breathe. Everything is so hard. I do not have anywhere to rest my legs, so I kick them; I keep moving them hard and out of order. There is no rhythm or grace in my paddling. I am trying to live!

The instructor was right beside me trying to get me to calm down. I simply couldn't calm. I was trapped in the deep end and no words would soothe me. I was a big distraction to the class and baffled the instructors. I catch glimpses of Faith sauntering over. She leaned down to talk with the two men, and they agreed taking me out of the pool would be safest for everyone. My instructor hopped out and offered me his hand. He pulled me up and Faith was there to retrieve my pieces. She had the look of disapproval on her face. I was so angry at her. Why didn't she hear that

I was afraid? I didn't have anything to prove to myself about swimming. I tried to please her but staying alive mattered more.

Why was it that I was always alone to deal with the hard moments of my life when she was around? She wasn't consoling or comforting. She was reticent and cold, just as her skin was cold during our last visit. She didn't have the comfort to lend. It wasn't her nature. She was protecting the one thing that mattered most in the world to her. Her pride. Even when her daughter needed to see a chink in her pride, she wouldn't buckle. The day in the pool showed me how to tread deep waters and live. If only I could have been given a life jacket for her funeral. I wasn't certain that my paddling skills would aid me in burying the last person in my lineage. The hero I loved. The mother I detested. The woman in- between. I needed a hand, someone to lift me from the deep waters and sinking memories of our history.

Faith always had a way of parading me around in her life. I was the living object she would pull from the bag of tricks and use to manipulate another unsuspecting person. This was what I told myself most of my life, after leaving the modeling agencies, the numerous theatre companies, dance lessons, or vocal training. All of which she would usually sign me up for and not be able to fulfill the financial obligation of. I was left feeling dejected, a failure.

She saw something in me that I didn't, or couldn't, see yet. She was trying everything she could to help me be known the in the world. She wanted to make something out of me. I didn't have the same desire. I was working very hard to not be seen. Especially by anyone that was male. I wanted to hide and be safe. Nothing was safe for me while I was in her care. I often felt like an object that was on display, tossed around and then put back on the shelf for the next hoopla.

It was a bad day at my new school. The kids had no interest in getting to know me. I sat alone per usual at lunch and wandered the long, eerie-feeling halls looking for my class. Why are all of the schools so big and terribly mismarked?

I walked home after a long day and waited in the motel room for Faith She was working at a motel and part of her compensation was free room and board. Living in a motel had its challenges; isolation, small space, no laundry room, always noisy, doors slamming. Yet it also was an adventur Soon after moving our few belongings into the motel, I met a girl and h brother. Their dad was working down the street for the automotive company. Jo was older than me, and her brother, Ed, was so cute! They both had black curly hair that completely mesmerized my eyes for hours. Each curl was defined, springy and its own character. Their bright smiles and genuine interest in getting to know me made living there tolerable. I felt that I belonged, if even for a moment.

When Faith came home, I begged her to take me for ice cream. "Please, mom, please. It's been a horrible day and I really NEED ice cream!" Maybe this is why I have been overweight my whole life? I NEED something to extinguish the pain, if even for a minute.

"Brigid, we are not going for ice cream. It's freezing cold outside, who would eat ice cream on a cold night?"

"I would," I said, continuing my pleas. She finally cracked and we were in the car. She drove a brown stick shift Gremlin. It seemed completely normal to me that a woman with one functioning arm would drive a stick shift. Did I also mention she was a smoker? I paid a lot of attention to the road because I was her gear shifter while she was puffing away on her Winston cigarette.

She looked tired, like the weight of the world rested on her shoulders. As we were cruising down the road, I was gazing at her profile. I loved the bridge of her nose, it was a perfect slope. Her big brown eyes always glistened, even if they were hidden behind bags. She began singing, *"Three blind mice, three blind mice, see how they run, see how they run. They ran after the farmer's wife, she cut off their dicks with a carving knife. Three blind mice."*

It wasn't until adulthood that I found the real lyrics for that song. At the time I was delighted. Most of her nursery rhymes had explicit lyrics. That was one of the things I found most charming about her—how the odd was normal.

When we arrived at Dairy Queen I ordered the usual: a peanut buster parfait with extra nuts. Oh, the delicious gooey-ness of that decadent treat! I stared at it for a moment to appreciate each layer and allow the saliva to build in my mouth.

As I began to dive in, "You know Brigid. Men love ice cream too."

"I'm sure mom; it's not just for girls!"

"No, I mean you are the ice cream and men LOVE ice cream. They will do anything to get it, anything! Do not let them have your ice cream, Brigid. Hold onto it until you are married."

I sat there with a perplexed look. Why would any boys try to take my ice cream? I was eight years old and she was my hero.

There were many escapades with motel living. Faith was often working or finding her own escapes. She preferred friends who could handle their liquor and chase said liquor with pills or cocaine. She lived a fast life and I was along for the ride. I learned at a young age that to have fun, it included booze. This particular night we were abundant with time and booze. I invited Jo down to my room. There were baskets littering the room filled with wine, champagne, and mini liquor bottles. I remember thinking at the time that these were strange gifts to be giving a young girl, since being the only child everything revolved around me. It never occurred to me that they may have been for another cause. Either way, they wouldn't make their final destination. Jo arrived and we quickly got to work, starting with a large bottle of Chardonnay. I hated it, it made my mouth dry and pucker, but we were having fun, weren't we? A few cigarettes in between, a dance party to The Doors, Billy Squire, and now to open the Cabernet. Yummy! This was much more pleasant.

Jo and I could talk for hours about our upbringing and how many places we lived. I, of course, had her beat by several apartments and miscellaneous homes. She was from Detroit, Michigan. The automotive industry there collapsed, and her Dad was lucky to find work here in Ohio. I was lucky, too, because without her company I would have been

even lonelier than I already was. She was at least four years older than m
she seemed worldly and mature. She "knew" things, and I was a sponge
curiosity. She taught me how to get free chips and pop from the hotel
vending machines, ways to sneak a mini pack of free cigarettes from the
hotel lobby, how to hop the train tracks to score marijuana in the project
how to break open the vending machines to get quarters... Not all of the:
were her sole idea; she had friends that "knew" more than her. None of
these antics seemed wrong; they were ways to eat up large chunks of time
I'd otherwise spend in my hotel room, alone. I was always up for the
adventure.

"Oh no, I am going to be sick!" Jo, laughing hysterically and stumbling
over to open the bathroom door, helped me in to hang my head in the
toilet. When my head was lifted it was Faith and she wasn't as amused as
Jo had been. She pulled me off the toilet, gave me tongue-lashings about
how irresponsible I was. She thought she could trust me, alone, with all o:
the booze. I checked the clock; it was 3:00 A.M.

The beautifully decorated baskets were door prizes for the fundraiser
they were hosting at her office. All in hopes of helping me: The girl who
tried to kill herself. Though I have zero recollection of such an event, I do
remember Faith asking me to wear wristbands for some time. "And if
anyone asks to see the marks, you tell them no." What marks? What are
you talking about? "Brigid just do as I ask." It was an odd request.

I was nine, there would be more....

Jo needed to see her guy over the tracks. It was late at night and I was
scared. This wasn't the first time we had been over the tracks, but it was
the first time at night. The tracks weren't the only obstacle. They were the
first-- the second and more difficult was crossing four lanes of traffic on
the highway. I wasn't an athletic girl, I was cushiony and soft.

Faith was hanging around a truck driver who had a dog that was part
wolf. He was more intimidating than this trek. As we were walking, this
was the first time I encountered conflict—I wasn't sure I should be doing
this. I wasn't certain that I would be ok, and I knew that Faith would be

looking for me, eventually. My steps were heavy, slow, and I began trailing behind the small pack of wolves that we were. There were a few boys that Jo knew, their names escape me. They were decent guys, hands off and only razzing here and there. None of them had an interest in me. I was too young and pudgy to be worth the risk. As I blew into my hands to keep them warm, my mind was racing. What if I can't make? What if we get caught buying drugs? What if they leave me behind? Will I know the way back at night? How will I tell Faith if anything should go wrong? Anxiety racing through me, I heard one of the guys call my name and usher me to catch up. I hurried my steps and soon we were facing the obstacles.

We hopped the tracks no problem. Luckily the trains seem to run more infrequently at night. As we approached the highway, my guts were in knots. Did I have what it took to make it all the way across without getting killed? We climbed the steep embankment, stood on the edge. One of the guys yelled down the line and said, "On my count, run like hell and don't look back, keep your eyes on me, the whole time!"

"OK!" we yelled back. He got into running position, just as a sprinter does in the Olympics. Bang! He was off! The next thing I knew I was already across two lanes, now to hop the median—except I couldn't hop it! I sat down and climbed over. Feeling accomplished, I looked up and everyone was on the other side of the highway screaming at me! I froze, like a deer in the headlights. This pattern has stuck with me the rest of my life. I still freeze when extreme fear takes over. It was noisy and hard to hear what they were screaming. I knew I had two choices: go back and find my way home alone or get my ass up and run like hell.

I ran and never looked back. I was now a part of the pack…

Uncle Gerry, who was Faith's younger brother, worked at the Holiday Inn, next door to our motel, The Budget Motor Inn. When things began to crumble at the Budget Motor Inn, we moved in with him. I was able to still see Jo and our pack. We spent many days hanging at the pool. The Holiday Inn was a big upgrade to our motel life. They had an indoor restaurant and bar, exercise room, and other amenities. It was at this hotel I learned how to steal from the vending machines, *back in those days you had a metal nail file and a couple of large paper clips you could get into most anything*, and sneak complimentary packs of Virginia Slims from the lobby desk. I dabbled with smoking at age 9; it was very exciting to join in the escapades of our small pack.

I had a Hot Lips Houlihan shirt that I wore almost daily. My body was often a battleground for my own self-abuse. I never enjoyed the way my landscape jutted out. My hot lips shirt helped me to feel taller and stronger than I felt on the inside. That shirt was pure magic! Army green with two huge lips across the chest, and M.A.S.H. 407 in block letters. The boys were beginning to notice me more as well. Our pack was changing. Jo and I were still close friends, but the boys we hung with were more distant these days. I didn't mind, it gave us time to plan our dreams for when we were older. The hotel days were wearing on me. Faith was partying harder than ever--- Uncle Gerry was the bartender and she took full advantage. I spent as much time away from the room as possible. It was quite cramped with the three of us living there, and it had a stale smell that the hotel air conditioner blew out.

Occasionally he would bring me gifts and try to make things as normal for a young girl as possible. By now this life was normal to me, but getting an Atari was exceptionally cool! I remember sitting in the room playing it for what seemed like days and being fixated on the challenges that the games Combat and Pitfall lent, while trying to win! This was my first exposure to being competitive.

One evening he came in very upset and had accused me of stealing his money. I never touched it, nor had I ever seen him so angry. Though I was sneaky and getting into trouble other ways, I respected him too much to take anything. I always suspected Faith did. She most likely couldn't remember the next day, unlike me. My ass was sore from the lashings I took from his belt! She stood by passively watching as if helpless. I needed a person who could keep me safe, and they were in short supply. Uncle Gerry was doing what he thought best to help a young lady toe the line. Taking a beating for something you didn't do was a hard lesson to swallow.

Luckily Jo was consistent in finding fun escapes for us. The newest was our entry into another hotel down the road that had an indoor pool. The indoor pool had port windows and anyone sitting in the bar could watch the people swimming in the pool. We had the grandest time playing with the customers in the bar. We would make funny faces, do underwater ballet, and if feeling especially frisky we would moon them and run as fast as we could out a back door. Our mischievous ways didn't catch up with us for many months until her friend was let go from the hotel and so went our free access pass.

Faith had an ever-changing shade of red hair, with large brown eyes that sparkled like a cloudless night. She was full of charisma. Faith was flamboyant in her attire and mannerisms. Her charisma is one of the things I loved most. With one look from Medusa you would be turned to stone; one look from Faith your wallet would turn inside out. She would walk into a room and everyone knew she was there. You may not have agreed with her views or mannerisms, but she worked hard to not be forgotten. Faith could read people and had a knack for playing on their sympathies.

Being in the shadow of that light was tough as an only child. I was often three steps behind her and called to the front when she wanted to show off her mini-me. I was a trophy that occasionally was pulled from the shelf. If she were here she may say otherwise, but this was how it felt. I didn't feel important all of the time, only on rare occasions. That was some of the strife between us. As I aged and came to understand how things worked with a little more maturity underneath me, I came to resent her mannerisms and the way she displayed me. I wanted to be her daughter, not someone she was proud of publicly and ignored behind the curtain. I was terribly lonely growing up. Anxiously awaiting her return, which most of the time I was disappointed because she would return too drunk to get the key in the door, or she would stumble through the door, giggling, with another guy on her arm. There were so many men in her life; she changed them like purses. I know she was looking to be loved. I could smell its rank odor in everything she did. She was hungry, we both were. If only we could have trusted each other to be enough.

She was raised by the ideology that a woman didn't amount to much if she were without a man. A man gave her status, authority, dignity. My mother didn't know she was a sovereign being. I believe she was afraid and lonely too. Even if she smiled, there was struggle ready to seep out. Life was hard for us; she worked a lot to provide food, shelter, and clothing. Many nights I would eat white bread smeared with ketchup because that was literally the best we had. She always found a way to pacify my needs and fulfill her own. I know that pills and cocaine are not cheap. She used one or a combination as often as possible. I was never quite sure which version of her I was being accompanied by. She had many personas; some were more tolerable than others. My least favorite was her martyr. I never asked to be born here; she chose to have me, knowing she would raise me alone. We didn't have a large family, and my grandmother was disgusted at my mother's choices. They, too, had a strained relationship. I imagine life may have been easier if Faith was seen as a stable woman who made good decisions.

Life was stacked against her at birth and she did it all. She lived, she laughed, and she loved. She died alone and I will always regret that. They say you can't control everything, that it's how you handle the circumstances. I try to not be too hard on myself for leaving her that night. I know my heart was sore and leaving was the only way I could breathe. I wasn't ready for her to die, and I wasn't ready to admit I needed more time. A clean slate, a way to erase all of the grime from our history. She was a woman. I am a woman. I understand now, things I couldn't be objective of back then. Maybe it wasn't my place to be objective. Maybe those were the years I was supposed to be with my angst and rage. Mom, if you hear me, I am sorry......

For a while, we lived in a house on Mortimer with Uncle Gerry and his girlfriend, who was my caregiver, and Faith's current flame, Vince. This house had an entire wall of cut out faces lined with velvet. If it's hard to imagine, it's harder to describe! It was psychedelic and unique. Gerry assured there was a responsible adult to care for me. This girlfriend had one shortcoming: she was a narcoleptic and would fall asleep at the most inconvenient times; driving me to school, before picking me up, or anytime in between. It made car rides extra anxiety provoking!

While there, Gerry and Faith also bred Doberman's. I would always get very excited when a litter was about to arrive. There was something so magical about seeing all of the little puppies fresh from the womb, and the loving care that their mother, Velvet, gave them. This was my first glimpse of the sacred!

The morning after we moved in, I excitedly ran out of the house. I wanted to be a part of a pack again. I saw the neighborhood kids gathered down the sidewalk a few houses. I quickly got dressed, grabbed my bike and ran up to them to introduce myself. They all looked at me with blank stares, and then one kid noticed I put my shorts on inside out and brought everyone else's attention to it. They laughed; I walked back to the house with my head hung low. *How is an awkward girl supposed to make friends, when she can't dress herself correctly?*

I attended co-ed Catholic schools from first through fifth grade. This event took place at St. Philip and James during the middle of second grade. We were in English class and Sister Claudiana had just finished the lesson. She asked each of us to go to the restroom and make sure to wash our hands. Janice and I went to the girl's room. We always traveled throughout the school with a buddy. The school was attached to a church, and occasionally there would be a service or viewing for a deceased parishioner. We never knew when this was going on so the nuns thought it best that we always have a friend with us. Oddly, we both were in the stall together. The steel blue of the bathroom stalls, coupled with the cool cinder block, always felt like I stepped into a cellar. The temperature, no matter how hot or cold outside, always left me with a numbing feeling. It had a creepy vibe. A few of the lights would flicker; several sinks were dripping.

Thankfully, the bathroom was filled with girls and their conversations distracted me from the ill feeling I had in the pit of my stomach. Janice and I were chatting about something silly, when all of a sudden the door was kicked open. We both looked at one another with complete terror, then back at the door. She screamed; I stood there in shock.

A grown man with a full beard opened his long coat and asked us, "Do you want to see my panties?" He was dressed in a cheerleading outfit, white with pink trim. It looked a little tattered and stained.

I watched in complete shock as Janice jumped off the toilet and blew past this man—girl—person and went screaming into the hallway. Her panties were still around her ankles by the time I caught up to her. We hugged one another and began to cry. It was a traumatic moment, as our walls of safety came crashing down.

We were rushed to the principal's office and asked hundreds of questions by the school staff and the police department. They decided the best thing for us was to leave school for a week. They asked our parents to seek someone to counsel us. Faith took me home and went back to work. I didn't see much of Janice that week. Being an only child was an isolating place for me to live. If I didn't have friends in the neighborhood where we landed, I often had to figure out a way to feel connected, most of the time I wasn't successful. My ways of entertaining myself were to watch TV, listen to albums, or read books.

In our house on Mortimer, I had a small stand up record player. There was a disco ball hanging from my ceiling and white transparent curtains on the windows. I had as many unicorn objects as I could fit all over my room; posters, ceramic figurines, snow globes, and my favorite pair of clogs. I would run around with them ALL DAY long! I loved the way they clippity-clopped on the floors. The sound reminded me of horses and a horse is close enough to a unicorn, so they, too, became instantly famous in my world.

After the panty caper, I began having nightmares. They weren't the usual variety, of being chased and running for your life. This one had a familiarity with it that made it hard to for me to separate from my reality.

At our school, there was a large cafeteria where the lunches were served daily. We would get to the cafeteria by walking down a long, dimly lit, hallway, followed by a small flight of stairs. It was always eerily quiet. You were offered a few choices of vegetable, protein, and bread. Every week without fail they would make creamed corn. It was served no matter what. I would constantly refuse to eat it, and they would force it onto my plate. That may not seem like a big deal, except that what went on the plate had to be in your belly before you were excused from the cafeteria. It wasn't honorable to waste. I would ask them to please not put it on my plate, and plop it went. My stomach would instantly begin to churn at the smell of it.

After forcing the slimy, stinky, and vilest of food combinations down my throat I would immediately run into the bathroom (without a buddy, no time for a buddy) and vomit. Every. Single. Time. Was that honorable?

In my nightmare, the same scenario played out, except for the plot twist: As I would be in the stall by myself, the entire bathroom would fill with blood. It would pour down the ceilings and rise from the floors. I couldn't get out of the stall because the door was welded shut. If I tried to escape through the small opening at the bottom of the door, I would have to go beneath the surface of the blood rising from the floor. I was terrified because I was trapped. The blood continued to flow in at a rapid rate, and then he would appear. This disfigured, man/creature thing that resembled Gollum from Lord of the rings. He was climbing all over the ceilings and walls, saying creepy things to me, and trying to entice me to come out of the stall. I realized that the stall was my harbor of safety because he couldn't get me in here! Still scared beyond my wits, I would press my body into a ball as tightly as possible on top of the toilet and begin to say Our Fathers.

Then I would awake in a cold sweat in my room, with the disco ball gleaming at me. Most nights I tried to curl up with my mom and feel her warmth next to me, to assure me it was only a bad dream. Some nights she wouldn't open her door, no matter how loud I banged and screamed. Eventually, I would fall asleep in a tight ball, wondering when I'd be assured it was only a bad dream.

A few weeks after the dust settled from Faith's passing, Nichol, my lifelong friend, stopped by to check in on me. Surprisingly, she brought me a similar placard as the one I left in the hospital. She was shopping and saw it and "just knew I had to have it." She was stunned to find out took one to Faith on Mother's Day, and that it wasn't there when I went to recover her belongings.

I had the inkling this was Faith working from the other side, similarly to what I was experiencing soon after her death...

I'd hear the phone ring, and when I answered, it was her.

"Hello?"

"Brigid, hi baby, it's me."

"Mom, why are you calling me?"

"I wanted to check in on you and see how you are."

"Mom, why are you calling me, you're dead!"

"Honey, I just want you to know that I am ok."

These calls went on for a good two months after her passing. I slowly began to accept that whatever this was, it was here to help me through my grief. I never expected to grieve her death. I was so attached to my anger, disdain, and pain that I didn't think grief had any chance of weaseling its way in. I was comforted by her phone calls. She seemed more apt to meet my needs in her death than in life. Perhaps it was easier to be herself without any pretense of who I needed her to be. That all faded with her last breath.

Each morning I wake to look at the placard, I still wait for the phone to ring.

"Going inward resurrects the soul." - Dr. Shefali Tsabary

Chapter Two
Faux Fathers

Happy thirteenth birthday to me! Today was going to be my day—finally—a day where the yelling and arguing would stop. A moment to feel normal, a state I wasn't used to feeling. I jumped out of bed, super excited to greet Faith and my step-dad of around two years, James. As I entered the dining room, no one was there. *Hmmm, that's odd. Oh! Maybe they're hiding in the living room to surprise me.* I tiptoe down the long hallway to find that the living room of red velvet furniture and medieval weaponry is empty. There's a note on the table: "Brigid, Happy Birthday, today was my early morning at work. Let's celebrate when I get home—Love, Mom."

That's it?! Her early day, so she left without saying goodbye? I felt devastated, crushed, alone. It'd been thirteen years hanging out with lonely and it never got easier. Lonely was my companion when all the real companions were taken. I made my way into the kitchen and made a quick breakfast.

By this time, we were settled in Lakewood, Ohio, a nice community with great schools and city services. I guess these things are important if you pay taxes, which I didn't. I was along for the ride, per usual. We lived in a three-bedroom apartment decorated in eclectic décor with a medieval flare, tall windows, and lots of space. The rooms were separated by a long hallway with a huge bathroom in between. Despite the shoddy cabinetry, our kitchen was spacious. This apartment felt roomy, a place to spread out after sharing a bedroom with Faith on and off while living with Bertha—and we had great neighbors. There were lots of kids of varying ages for me to play with.

This was the home where pivotal development took place. I blossomed into a young woman in this apartment. I met my first love and was violated by my step-dad. All the shit went down in this apartment. Maybe it's not a coincidence that it was burned down years after we left? It had a heaviness that none of us could shake.

Today was my day; I would celebrate being an official teenager. I mean I still felt 12, not any different, but a milestone had been reached—one that the other kids seem to make a big deal about. I readied myself for school and walked my way there. I lived about 2.5 miles from the school and each day was an adventure, never knowing what I would see along the way. I saw men masturbating in the car while stopped at a red light, some with a towel over their laps, others not as modest. I would hear domestic disputes or kids crying. That always felt familiar and comforting. My step-dad was a violent alcoholic. He wasn't physically threatening to look at, but one glance his way and my skin would crawl. He swept Faith off her feet. I could feel her heart soften for him. She was finally rescued of her loneliness. Now she had a husband and partner. Except that he needed a punching bag, not an equal.

Sometimes I would see a deer or colorful bird, something to break up the counting of my steps. I did that to help the time pass, and to keep my mind on one thought. I had a lot of anxiety and running thoughts. Fear, loneliness, and not belonging hung around my throat every second. I just didn't know how to blend in at my school or find a peer group that "got" me. I knew kids in our apartment complex but didn't have a lot of friends at school. It was a large school, the biggest I had attended to date. I wasn't intimidated by the size. There was a certain type of peacefulness to being anonymous amongst the faces. Some of the kids were familiar because I had met those two years earlier in middle school. I just hadn't found a tribe of people.

I arrived at school and smiled brightly. Today was my day and I would celebrate, no matter what. I told the security guard, a few teachers, my friend Kristen, and a few other random people that today were my birthday.

"Happy Birthday! What are your plans tonight?" they asked.

"I am not sure, my mom had to work early and she said we'd celebrate later in the evening." My mind wandered all day, what would we do, would we go out, stay in? Who would be there? I hope she ordered a cake. I love cassata cake. Yes! That would make it a fun way to celebrate.

Losing my penchant for ice cream after the "ice cream sex talk", cake an Twix bars quickly became my replacements.

I watched the clock all day at school. Finally, it rang 3:30 and I bolted out the door, walking home as briskly as possible. When I arrived, James was home, with a cracked Schlitz being drunk.

The air is densely filled with cigarette smoke. I hear Hank Williams blaring in the dining room. Someone was partying! Faith hadn't arrived yet. I went into my room and locked the door and worked on some homework to keep a low profile. His drinking kept me on edge. I never knew which beer would be the one to send him to his dark place. Not knowing how long he'd been home, or how many cans were emptied, my room was the safest place for me.

About 4:30 Faith arrived and was walking through the apartment calling my name. She seemed happy today. I came out of my room and she had balloons. I love balloons! She had a few wrapped gifts and said that my cake was in the refrigerator. YAY! This day was improving every minute. She went into the kitchen and began preparing dinner. As she was clanking around with the pots, she asked how my day was. *Did I have any surprises at school? Did I complete my homework? What was my wish for my 13th birthday?*

What was my wish for my 13th birthday? I hadn't even thought about that!

"Oh, I know. But If I tell you it won't come true."

"Oh, Brigid. That is an old wives tale."

"Yes, but it came to be known because some parts of it must be true. I don't want to share my wish; I will think it when I blow out my candles."

I asked her how she spent her 13th birthday. She took a long pause and went back to cooking. I never did hear stories about her upbringing. It wasn't until her passing that I came to know more of the woman I called mom.

There was a knock at the door.

"I'll get it!" I called out. As I rushed to the door, I was full of excitement at who would be on the other side. I peeked through the peephole, an old habit from our motel days. The distorted face looking back at me through the fisheye lens was one I didn't recognize.

There stood a tall man with wiry red hair and crazy eyes. I put the chain on the door and slowly began to open it. Through the crack, I saw that the man was holding a carton of cigarettes and jug of wine.

"Happy 13th birthday Brigid," he said. "I'm your dad."

I stood there taking in the sight of what was happening before my eyes.

"Oh," I said and slammed the door. "Mom? There is a man claiming to be my dad at the door..."

I knew this man was mistaken because my dad died in a horrible car accident. That was the story I clung to my whole life. I knew it to be truer than true, because if he were alive, why would he wish to be dead in a horrible car accident after missing most of my growing up?!

I stood at the door, my heart racing, thoughts flooding my mind. *Who is this man, why does he think he is my father? He knows it's my 13th birthday. How does he know that? How does he know my name? I've never seen this man before. What is going on?*

The door was opened all the way and this stranger invited in. Faith put his gifts (if you can call a carton of cigarettes and wine gifts for a young lady) on the table and introduced him as Chad. Chad had just been released from maximum security prison (for what I can only assume was a hideous crime) 13 years ago! He said he'd been anticipating this moment his whole stay in prison that he couldn't wait to meet his daughter, take her home to meet his mother and father, that I have a whole other side of the family waiting to meet me.

Why? Why did he care so much about my birthday? I could sense the tension that was mounting. James was standing next to Faith, she was whispering to him. Chad was looking around like a toddler in a house of glass. Everything caught his attention and he was frozen in place. Time slowed to a ticking pulse. I could feel every second click off the clock. These seconds will never come back. This is life falling away, with each tick an tock, more disappears forever. I was paying attention with my eyes, but my mind was racing, I couldn't feel my toes. I felt as though I was hovering above the situation, it was startling, and I need a safe place to retreat.

I found this walking hiding spot the night I was raped at Cole's house. He was a biker and ran with wild characters. His crew was full of single men who liked booze, drugs, and women. Unfortunately, I wasn't a woman, I was a child, but once the feel-goods kicked in, the shroud of n innocence fell away and was left on the floor next to my stained panties blood and semen. I found a way to watch the incident without feeling it. would hide out of my body, not too far. Just enough to keep it moving, but the feelings were distant. I felt safe here. As safe as I could get, without any authority or strength. I had to find a place to hide because li around me was chaos.

I never enjoyed learning or having to go to school. I went because I knew that for those minutes I would be fed, and I would be safe. No one was looking to pull another petal from my blossom of innocence. There i could stay in the water, unhampered or harmed.

I could hear all of them talking. Faith's face was quite distressed. She wa mediating between James and this Chad character. Why was James upset? He didn't have anything to do with this. Yet, Chad seems to know him Chad was reciting a story about when the two of them were in the Pen together. WHAT!! I never knew this. Chad and James were in the same cell block. James was corresponding with Faith while serving his sentence. How did she find this guy? Why did she settle for him? He was a scumbag and brought a plague upon our lives. Now one of his cellmates is here claiming to be my dad?! This is a weird day. I turned back to what was happening and they were packing up. They decided to take this talk elsewhere. I hunched over with the heft of disappointment that fell upon me. I would be spending the rest of this day alone.
Happy 13th Birthday Brigid, your presumed dad has arrived gift boxed for you!

There is a small amusement park in Cleveland called Memphis Kiddie Park. It has several rides for small children. I remember being there with a friend of my mother's named John. He was a tall man, with long brown hair, a neat mustache, and kind eyes. He walked me through the park and held my hand the whole time. I was instantly comfortable with him. Faith had several men in her life; she changed them as swiftly as the seasons. Most were off-putting, and I never wanted anything to do with them. This may have had more to do with me and feeling that I had to compete for her attention, or it may have been good instincts on my part. Faith was hungry to belong to someone, anyone but me. Only a man would complete her. I can still feel the insipid taste in my mouth when I speak that. It wasn't for me to complete her, if only she knew that we belonged to one another.

John was kind and gentle, and he listened to me. I could talk on and on, he would patiently listen with a soft smile, and then ask a question that invited more talking. I can still see us at Kiddie Park; me holding his hand, looking up at him. Him looking down at me, with pure love. The rides were buzzing with lights and chimes, kids were playing and laughing. He was wearing a red and black plaid shirt. He was a modern cowboy of sorts. He had a Midwestern style, with a Cleveland soul. A little grit, blue collar, family-oriented spirit to him. A family man understood that listening was important. If you come from a big family, you know how some voices will trump others. I wondered if he came from a big family. I know I asked him many questions about who he was, and where he came from. If time were kind it would let me remember all of the finite details. The feelings I felt were confusing for me, the level of comfort I felt in his company. He felt like a father to me, but my dad died in a car accident. I battled between wanting to hold on and knowing I had to let his hand go because he wouldn't last, they never did. I wanted him to stay. We needed him to stay. One good man to stay and remind us that we were enough, both of us, not just Faith. I needed my Dad....

The story went like this: *Brigid your dad loved us very much. You were still a baby. Too young to remember him. He was driving home one night and there was a collision. Your dad was hit by a semi and didn't make it. He was killed instantly and didn't feel any pain. He loved you. I know he is watching over us.* When I think about the story, it often comforted me to know that I had a daddy who loved me. He would be here if he could. The story helped me when the kids at school would ask about my Dad. Every Father's Day, father-daughter dance, my birthday—I knew that my dad was watching over me. They say it's all about the details. I hadn't doubted her story about my father until I met Chad. The little things in her story started to blink in red. *Why didn't I know my Dad's name? Why didn't she tell me how old he was? Why didn't I know his side of the family?* Chad had arrived with a plan; he was ready to assume full responsibility for me. He was eager to take me home and claim me as his kid. *Why didn't I know my grandparents from my Dad's side of the family?* She never spoke of them, or if he had any siblings. He was a ghost in every sense, a mythical story that would live as long as she told it.

Just as I had done in Catholic school, I began to ask a lot of questions. Questions that, when answered, left me more dissatisfied than when I began. Faith didn't know the answers and so she left it to "faith." *Just believe. Just trust. We can't always know things in order to believe in them.* Bullshit! If you loved my father and were married to him, how could you not know the simplest answers to my questions? I know as much as I can remember about my own husband's side of the family; details about where they emigrated from, his grandparents, their children, etc.... Everyone has a history. I couldn't understand why his was so uninteresting to her that she never asked!

I give Chad credit; he was ready to enact a plan that would help me feel that I belonged to someone. That I mattered, and they had an interest in getting to know me. The next few weeks of his visit were hard for me and Faith. I began to distrust her more than I already did. I questioned everything that I once took at face value. I didn't care anymore about how it made her feel. Did anyone stop to ask how it made me feel? I learned at an early age to take care of myself. I always had to consider my own survival needs. I was walking to school every day at the age of eight. That may not seem like a big deal, but I had to do this walking along a road that was filled with strip clubs, hotels, and motels. I was eight years old walking alone, about 2-3 miles each way, to attend third and fourth-grade school.

One of the substitutes in my life was Vince, a tall statured man with sunken eyes, straight posture, and light-colored hair. He seldom looked at me. His attention was always on Faith. Maybe they were in love if that is what love looked like. Vince liked to keep me at a distance. I was nothing more than a nuisance. I often felt uncomfortable around him, and angry at Faith for leaving me alone with him. He had an air about him that kept all of my senses on heightened alert. It was during the time of the Panties Escapade that we lived with Vince. He convinced Faith to keep their bedroom door locked. Many nights after waking from the horrific nightmare of the school's bathroom, I would lay against the door, crying for my mother. Why did he deserve more of her than me? Even if he was a nice man, my younger self couldn't see it. I still grapple with his motives and influence, more so the abandonment I constantly felt.

We were waiting in line at McDonald's; I didn't want anything but an ice cream cone. Faith refused to buy me ice cream because by this age I was getting more round than tall. She would remark that "pretty girls don't need ice cream all of the time." "Skinny girls get the best husbands." "You wouldn't want to miss out on a great guy because of this ice cream cone."

I was around 10 years old, I couldn't care less about the potential man I would meet 15 years from now. I wanted a cone, NOW!

She mumbled something to Vince, he looked down at me. My eyes darted between the two of them. I was in eager anticipation of my cone. He paid for everything, the cashier offered him the cone, and he looked down to pass it over to me. I looked at him with a glare and crossed my arms together.

"NO thank you, Vince. I asked Faith to buy me a cone. I don't want a cone from you, only her."

Faith looked over at me, with a deviant smile. "You want the cone only from me?" she asked.

"Yes, I don't like him, and I don't want anything from him," I replied.

"Ok Brigid. Here you go!" and she shoved the cone right in my face.

Part of it clung to my nose. You could hear the rest plop on the floor. The room got quiet and I felt the uncomfortable stares of the other patrons.

She turned to Vince and said, "Let's go."

He pranced out behind her. I stood there in awe of what just took place.

Too embarrassed to be mad, I pulled the cone from my nose with tear-filled eyes and asked for napkins. The cashier asked me if I wanted another cone. "Sure," I said.

I wiped myself off and went outside to catch up with them. She was furious that I was given another cone. Jokes on you Faith, I know how to get what I want.

I have a muddled memory of me, Vince, and Faith being at Grandma Bobo's apartment. She and Vince were in the bedroom giggling and whispering about something. Vince came back into the living room and asked me if I would like to learn how to kiss.

"No. Why are you asking me this?"

"Your mom thinks it's a good idea if I help you with this."

"Why are you asking him to teach me, Mom?"

"Brigid, just let him help you!"

I was shaking and didn't want any part of him touching me. He always gave me a bad feeling inside. He asked me to rise to my feet. I looked over to my Grandmother, who was wincing. Vince made his way to me and stood above me.

"Stand up Brigid, we want to make your mother happy."

Standing on wobbly legs, I looked up at him, and he reached down towards me and planted a kiss on my lips. I ran into the bathroom, hysterically crying. I never went near him after that moment.

Bobo despised any man Faith brought to her home, most especially Vince. Each time they dropped me off, Faith would remind me to stand to the side, because Bobo inevitably threw an ashtray at him! I gotta give it to her; she made no pretense to like someone she didn't.

When I was in Catholic school, I remember having to go to confession weekly in order to receive the Eucharist. What I really called it was the sticky circle. I was fascinated by how it clung to the roof of my mouth. I had different strategies that I theorized and then tested week after week. No matter how much saliva, tongue assistance, or air I kept in my mouth, the sticky circle would adhere to the roof my mouth, like a hungry octopus, and I would spend the rest of the mass trying to pry it off.

James most likely never attended mass or confession, for the sins of his heart ran deeper than the Amazon River. He was a tortured man, and Faith fell head over heels for him. Finally, someone who could relate to her suffering. The first time I met him, I knew that we would have a hard life ahead. He reeked of alcohol and cigarettes. His eyes were a steely blue that pierced through me every time he glanced in my direction. His pupils were little beady scanners, laser-like.

He had a gruff voice and posture—an air about him that said *I've lived a rough life and my closet is full of secrets.* He didn't have any soft edges; he hid his smile as well as his thoughts. The only time James shared what he was feeling was through anger.

Faith and James met when I was completing my fifth year of education. We were living with an elderly woman in our neighborhood at the time, Bertha. Bertha took me in shortly after the final ambulance was at our home, a few houses down from hers. That was the third or fourth time the ambulance had come for me. She never asked me about what took place at Cole's house. I was thankful for the favor. I wasn't ready to talk about it. She was hesitant to let Faith in, but eventually she opened up her home to her as well, despite her family's outcry.

Bertha had a strong repulsion toward James just as I had, and wasn't to fond of Faith, either. He and Faith had decided that it would be best for me to live in a community with a good school system. I had asked to attend public school, as I didn't necessarily agree with the teachings of th Catholic school I was attending. A lot of what I was exposed to didn't make sense to me and I was tired of pretending to belong to something I didn't even understand.

We moved to a city called Lakewood. The day we were moving from Bertha's home felt like I was being ripped from the womb. Her home wa my haven, the first place I felt safe and cared for since the passing of my grandmother, Bobo. Bertha had a tenderness to her that I could sink into I never felt guarded or worried that something would be different. She was my new steady.

The house down the street, that I'd come from, was a drug house, and there was always commotion taking place there. It was seldom quiet or peaceful. There were often men in and out, who were large, loud, and stunk. They didn't come to socialize, they came to party. The owner of the house, Cole, was a dealer; he sold marijuana and cocaine. The basement of the house was filled with animals and I never did understand why he kept them. The house had a steady cloud of smoke that hung in every room. It made the lighting look like a fog light trying to pierce a foggy night. I tried to stay in my room as often as I could while living there.

Faith was more distant than usual. She would be gone all day and come home at odd hours of the evening. I remember one night she was gone and I was curled up in my room. There was fighting taking place between Cole and one of his guests. I just kept praying that Faith would come back and we could leave this place for good.

I must have dozed off as I awoke to a light knocking on the door.

Tap, tap, "Biiiiiigiiid," in a whispered voice.

Tap, tap, "Briiiiiigiiiiidd, baby come help me get into the door." Tap, tap, tap.

I rubbed my eyes, opened the door to my room. The lights were on, and music was playing in the back room. There was a man lying on the tan velour chair in the living room, one leg hung over the armrest. I crept to the door, so as to not wake this man, and there was Faith, fiddling with her key and wobbling back and forth at the door. She appeared to be alone and was talking to herself. Laughing and cursing about how the damn key wouldn't stay steady. She was the one rocking back and forth. I left the chain on the door, and slowly opened it.

"Briiiigiiiid, there you are baby, let me in."

"NO." I said.

"Whaaaat?" she asked, with a long drawl.

"No, I'm not letting you in." Her eyes were glazed over, not even able to focus on me. There was a rage festering inside of me. I was completely disgusted with her! *Why would she be this messed up and look to me to help her in?* I closed the door and crept slowly back to my room.

During this time, Faith was partying and hanging out a lot with a tall and slender man with dark hair. Her belly started getting bigger, but she told me nothing was wrong if I said anything. I knew about babies, but in my mind, she was too old to be pregnant.

A month or two after I moved in with Bertha, Faith went to the hospital to have "cancer surgery." She returned to Cole's a few days later before finally being allowed to move in with us. When we moved to 117th with James, I stumbled upon paperwork that revealed that she'd given up a baby boy for adoption. When I asked about it, she denied it.

When I met Adam's father, Robert, I was instantly charmed. He had a quick wit and shimmering blue eyes that were accentuated by his grey hair. Standing at six feet tall, he held a presence that I can only assume he was unaware of. He reminded me of a more handsome version of Ernest Hemingway, sea captain-esque, tinged with mystery and darkness. Adam's family had many stories of how Bob would yell all the time. He subsequently lost his voice due to throat cancer and was now only able to speak with the use of an Electro larynx, which would frustrate him to no end. I too, would be frustrated if I had to change a battery to a device, my only way of speaking, in the middle of a discussion! It would be maddening. Somehow everyone gave grace and patience even when he had none of his own to give.

He grabbed me after Adam and I were engaged and said: "Brigid the smartest thing my son ever did was ask you to be his wife." That simple statement meant the world to me! I wanted his approval more than anything. He seemed impenetrable; hard to chip away at his outer layer of disdain for most of humanity. He loved dogs—people, not so much. Maybe it was his years of teaching in one of Cleveland's most hostile High Schools.

He was a teacher of Physics and Computer Science. With genius level intelligence, he was invited to be a part of Mensa. The man built his own sailboat during his spare time in the summers. Ellen (Adam's mother) would get violently sea sick, and Adam didn't like the spiders. The building of the boat was most likely more satisfying then setting sail.

I still have some of his drawings, as that was also a passing passion for him. He explored many of his creative outlets, his most favored was drinking. Bob loved baseball and cold beers. It was who he was. He also made ridiculously good Blue Margaritas, which buoyed our young Alex in the sac—unbeknownst to me—I was in the early weeks of pregnancy when I overindulged on Bob's Blue Margarita's.

His later years came with the birth of several grandchildren, followed by his declining health. His hard shell began to soften. Watching the patriarch of the family decline was a slow and difficult process, one that made me long for his persnicketiness to return. It never did, and we spent the last year of his life in silent conversations. I would go to their home every two weeks or so and trim Bob's hair, beard, and nails. He would sit quietly, with a small grin on his face, receiving the affections I offered. I would watch him, wondering where he was with his thoughts. *What mattered most to him? What brought his heart peace?* I never asked. He never shared. He would wince every time I went to cut his nails. It made me chuckle, he just never trusted me to clip them. Fearing I would nip his skin, though I never did, he still jumped. It was quite funny to watch, irritating to be involved with. I would bark at him, he would snap at me. Then we would go back into silence. The grin, now a grimace, and me still wishing for his approval.

I see glimpses of Adam in Bob, some more comforting than others. Adam is a genius. He too becomes restless with life, and systems.

It wasn't his job to give me something my own father never did, a place to be restful with whom I was as a daughter, a woman, the counter to his masculine strength. Bob wasn't always easy, but he was the closest I had to a Dad as an adult. I am glad we had those silent conversations. Rest in peace Bob, I miss you.

Chapter Three
Trauma Road

My strength isn't in what I endure. My strength is in what I allow to come fully into my being, feeling all of it with non-attachment to an outcome or result.

I Always wanted to be like the athletic kids… Self-assured. Physically strong. Confident. Dedicated. Parents who waited for them in the car line after school, with big smiles and a freshly baked after-school snack anticipating their arrival. Parents who attended every game and cheered them on from the stands!

They seemed to have a lot going for them. I made assumptions about how glorious their life is, as I had a lot of time on my hands watching from the sidelines. Who am I? Well, I am the chubby awkward kid with ill-fitting clothes, frizzy hair, and a crooked smile. Though many people don't see that it's crooked because I more or less grin than smile.

Mother always told me I'd be prettier if I lost a few pounds and smiled more. I bet their mothers don't suggest they need to lose weight. I'm even betting their mothers praise them for things far more important than being pretty. She would say, "You would have more friends and be popular if only you were thinner." "Oh, I know, yes, I know what you need, you need new clothes. Yeah, yeah! That will help, that's exactly what you need!" Mother had all kinds of fancy ideas about why I wasn't chosen.

I was quiet and observant during my younger years. I lacked self-confidence and pizzazz. I simply wanted to get by, hoping one day I would get out of the confines of these systems. I was a poor student, spending most of my learning time daydreaming about the wild adventures I would have as a freshly graduated adult.

Fast forward a few frames, and I am standing outside with my hands gripping a Styrofoam cup, sipping warm coffee with powdered creamer, letting the steam warm my face, chatting with complete strangers. There are no sidelines here. It's us against the grim reaper. We are all fighting a battle that no parent should ever face, let alone many. Each of our children is here for life-threatening illness or abnormalities. What cleaved my memories was mutuality. Our pain created a bridge that left behind any pretenses, social classes, popularity, and status. We were parents who deeply love our children. Floating in a dream of surreal expression; nurses' doctors, volunteers, always talking at us, checking the tubes, noting the pace of the beeps. Each person had a job to do, niceties were a commodity. My early years of being rejected actually helped me greatly in my later years. I've learned how to handle pain and adversity.

I remember one girl I envied in school. Her name was Bridget with an "et", mine is with an "id". People would often confuse us because we had the same sounding name. I mean really, what were the chances? One night we were at a Halloween party. She was there with her group of popular kids; I was there with the so-called misfits. I noticed her big seemingly perfect smile and wavy hair from across the room. She had the most beautiful hair, she really did, and it flowed and bounced, and always looked so perfect and well-tended. She had a carefree, seamless air about her—that life handed her the golden cup. Mine was more of a dwarf-sized Dixie Cup with several creases. I was moving about the crowd with a smitten grin, one that politely spoke: I know who you people are and the lives you live. I detest your innocence, your ease.

As I made my way to the ladies' room, Bridget was there. She said hello to me and we shared idle conversation. Several beers later and another round in the bathroom, she started spilling all the details. She was miserable. Her parents separated, and she neither confirmed, nor denied the rumors I had heard of her best friend's family was in the process of adopting her! She was living a facade and was sad of the way life was rolling along for her. My mouth was wide enough that a toad could pop out. I mean, how could this be? She has the perfect hair, social circle, and smile. She's so popular and everybody loves her. And, she had to hide from who she really was, what she was really going through. Her group put a lot of pressure on her to perform. Similarly to my mother, she always had an agenda and goal in mind for how I would win the game— how I could manipulate the score to get ahead.

That night showed me to slow down with making assumptions, to noti that everything isn't always as it appears. Many are running from some shadow, or clutches of shame. It perplexes me that as a society we run s far away from holding pain. When pain crops up, there's an automatic response to flee or stomp it out. As a culture, there is little taught in our schools or businesses on how to safely support and hold pain with another person. I was often in pain as I stood on the sidelines. I felt lone and isolated, not sure where I fit in or if I belonged. Faith repeatedly proved this scenario correct with her assertions that I needed to do more in order to be more. Standing alongside another in their pain, even with my own, may be a skill that takes a lifetime to master, and I can't think of any learning more worthy of my attendance.

When our daughter was in the NICU, to keep sane while she was resting I would take a 15-minute break every few hours. The outside courtyard was the first time I was shown how to hold pain, and where I was accepted. Nothing else mattered. There wasn't time to pretend. We had minutes to be known, understood and supported, before going back into the unknown, literal minutes. Each person I met, offered softness, tissues, and more coffee. We even found ways to laugh or be comforted in the silence of an early morning gathering. *The traumas one experiences send a shockwave to the system that can take years to settle the ripples. Being in survival mode helps you deal with what is right in front of you without any pretense that you understand, or realize the full weight of the circumstance. It's a foggy reality that clears with time, and tears.*

She had undergone two open-heart surgeries within seven days. The entire process was gut-wrenching and showed me that any part of me that I thought couldn't make it, excelled. We handed over our 18-month-old girl to a medical team we had been supported by since she was four months in utero. During our first ultrasound, they had discovered she only had three chambers to her heart. Everything about that day is slowly making its way to resting peacefully in our memories. The reason we made it through the pregnancy, birth, and now these surgeries was one simple thing (I know, it seems trite to lay someone's life on any one *simple* thing and I do not say this in gest): our daughter gave us a thumbs-up during her ultrasound, the very first time I saw our little baby. Her sex was to be revealed on the delivery day. There were her tiny fingers giving us a very clear, unmistakable thumbs-up. I looked at Adam and said, "Isn't that amazing, she is giving us a thumbs-up!" Little did I know how amazing that moment really was, and how far it would take us.

Every doctor told us the baby wouldn't live to delivery. We went in for dozens of tests, only to leave each one feeling more defeated than the last. The prognosis and diagnosis kept getting worse. I never knew the human body could produce so many tears until we lived through those grueling weeks. From the time they discovered the birth defect, to the time I would no longer be legally allowed to terminate, was a total of 16 days. How in the world can an expectant mother be told she has 16 days to decide the fate of her child, and family? When I asked what could have caused this, worrying that it was a child defect from the Zoloft I was prescribed for postpartum depression after my son was born, the first doctor told me it most likely was because I was overweight. Whether or not that is true, is it really the best way to approach a panicked pregnant woman? The guilt was endless, the shame consuming.

Each day Adam and I wept, consoled, sobbed, and slept. We showed up to every appointment with a new whisper of hope in our hearts -- remembering our little baby gave us a thumbs-up -- only to leave feeling the tears return.

When we had two days left, I received a phone call while Adam was teaching. The woman introduced herself and spoke of this doctor and her role, and how they created an appointment for us because, looking through our chart, they could see we were up against a wall, time was running out. Although to be honest, I never felt that I would go through with terminating the pregnancy. We were bonded, and I was committed to meeting our child at all costs. When we met Donna, she was a ray of sunshine. She beamed with all the hope we left behind. She assured us that Dr. Patel was the leader in pediatric cardiology across the country. If anyone could help us, it is him. He sees only the incredibly high-risk cases, and unbeknownst to us, we were one of those cases. I can thank being naive and frightened for relieving us of just how dire our circumstances really were. We knew things were bad, I just never allowed how bad, to fully penetrate my consciousness.

After several hours of having multiple tests run, we sat in a brightly lit room, with a low-grade hum from one of the neon lights. Adam and I were exhausted and scared. We knew that this would be our last round o testing. We would know the fate of our baby.

Dr. Patel drew a marvelous picture of our situation. He drew our daughter's heart and explained that she had an Atrioventricular Septal Defect (AVSD), and Heterotaxy (her internal mirroring was backwards, leaving her organs in a different location or position). There are three chambers to her heart; her long-term prognosis without surgery to repair her heart would be bleak. She would have a poor quality of life because she wouldn't be getting enough oxygen in her blood. The best he could offer would be a lifespan of up to 5-7 years of age. The blue blood wasn't mixing efficiently with her red blood. Also, that the genes that form the heart were disrupted during her development. One of the DNA strands had been nipped right on the corner of one gene, which threw everything out of whack, her patterning was off. Her heart rests cockeyed and her internal organs are backward, most everything was where it needed to be, but in a newly organized way. They looked for a long time trying to find her spleen, with no success.

He gave us the good, bad, the ugly. Overall, he was hopeful and I could feel my air beginning to move again within my body. The game changer was the two valves exiting the heart. They needed to be in the right place, but every other anomaly could be dealt with. They could give her surgery before the age of two, which would assure she would have a quality of life and normal growth—assuming that all went as intended during the surgeries. For the first time in weeks, we felt that we could breathe.

This was all happening as we were trying to care for her older brother, who was six months old. Adam was working full time and attending graduate school. Life felt lonely and hard. I had so much room around me; it was as if everyone and everything around us took two steps back. I suppose this was helpful, but it felt like too much space. I needed to be held, as I was literally carrying the fate of life in my belly. I wasn't prepared for a balanced way of dealing with all that was in front of us. I was trying to survive. Every minute ticked and my mind was ladened with worry. Adam was my anchor and helped to keep things in a logical, rational place. He was able to separate his emotion which did help us to have productive conversations. All I could do was cry. I never knew how long a person could cry for, until now. Every day, countless times throughout the day, I was walking through life in slow motion. I felt like a plastic bag from the grocery story floating on currents of air. Not quite landing, coming close and being pulled backward again or cast forward. I just kept floating and listening and crying and talking and crying.

Her missing spleen created a different scenario. She would need to be on antibiotics her entire life to help her immune system. That didn't sound good to us because we know that the body can become resistant to antibiotics, and at some point, she would run out of immune support. I had dreams for this baby and none of them included half of her lifetime in the hospital or living in a bubble. To me that isn't living, it's a cage.

Dr. Patel suggested we go home, eat, rest and allow all of the information to settle. He offered us a follow-up appointment in two days. We gladly accepted his offer. We spent the next 48 hours going over every potential what if... Let's face it, there are many that we could never have considered. Our biggest ones were *what if she can't play outside, or have friends be near her? What if she is immunocompromised and ends up on IV antibiotics to keep her alive? What if she does have Down's syndrome or any of the other countless potential anomalies they had thrown at us? What if one of the earlier doctors was right? Can we leave our child in a home to finish her life, if we were to pass away before her? What if she could never play sports, ride a bike, swim, etc.?*

When we entered Dr. Patel's office, my mind was certain, and my heart was beating out of my chest. I held Adam's hand so hard it was turning purple. I was ready to hear whatever he had to say, and it wouldn't change my mind. Nothing at this point would sway me. I was definite. She gave us a sign, I know that was her communicating with us that everything will be ok.

During our consultation with him, he suggested doing another ultrasound and asked me to drink a lot of water, A LOT of water. Then the fun came in that I couldn't relieve myself. I had to fill my bladder to help with the imaging. He was determined to find her spleen. He had thought about her Heterotaxy, how everything was juxtaposition.

As I lay on the table, every push of the little wand was torturous. I mean what was this man, a sadist? After about thirty minutes he called Adam over, excitedly. They both were *uhh, mmmhmm, yep, yes I see it!* I was about to pop! Do you remember Violet Beauregard in Willy Wonka, the girl who loved gum? She stole a piece of gum that turned her into a blueberry and she kept growing and growing. Yes, I was her progeny!

At last, Dr. Patel offered for me to use the restroom, and when I returned he and Adam were standing there with gleeful smiles. *What is it? Why are you both so happy? Did you find her spleen? YES! We found it, and it's in great health, it is on the other side of her body, but it's working.* Back to the tears. This time they were tears of joy! This little baby continues to surprise us with her perseverance.

We were on a spring wildflower trail when I began having contractions. It was the three of us; me, Adam, and Alex, enjoying the warmth of the sun, the decorated trail of spring beauties.

"Adam, I think I'm going into labor."

"Right now?!"

"Yes, honey, right now." We hurried home, called the doctor and began our drive to Akron. That was where the high-risk delivery team would greet us. My contractions grew, and I knew soon we would be meeting our baby.

During my delivery with Alex, I was set on it being 100% natural. I had a water tub, soft music, aromatherapy, and my midwife. It was a peaceful environment. I remember begging them to not make me leave the water. Its warmth was calming and helped with my contractions. I was on and off of labor with him for about 38 hours. At one point we were asked to go home and rest. I drank cod liver oil and played with my boobs to help stimulate the contractions! The day before his delivery I was watching "A

Baby Story" on TLC, dreaming of what it would be like. Each of the moms on that show made delivery look seamless.

Instead, I was like a greased hog, trying to flee the pen! No grace, only screams, and squealing. After hours of trying it au naturel, they encouraged me to get an epidural and Pitocin to stimulate stronger contractions and help me to fully dilate. My water broke several hours before and I wasn't making quick enough progress. If option one didn't work, they wanted me to have a C-section.

I do believe that our body knows when and how to deliver a child. But I was in a hospital and they have a completely different rhythm they follow. Adam and I discussed all our options. I could do Pitocin and epidural, or C-section. I chose the epi. I wasn't ready to get a C-section, fearing I would never be able to give birth naturally again. It turns out that a C-section most likely would have been our best choice. We didn't know or couldn't have predicted that our boy was too big for my pelvis and would get stuck in the canal. I remember the scared looks on everyone's faces. The nurse and our midwife each took a hip and pushed down to help Alex come through the canal. I was literally torn up. I had a level four episiotomy and numerous stitches. He fought hard to come into this world! Holding our little boy was a surreal experience. I was flushed with emotions and only remember staring at him in awe.

I'm still healing from that birth trauma, and here we are in the high-risk delivery section of the hospital, awaiting the delivery of our baby (we still didn't know the sex).

Adam and I walked the halls, (*there would be no soft music or water during this delivery*) joked around and did everything we could to keep the contractions strong. It came to the time that I needed rest, and I asked for an epidural. That request caused many problems between Adam and me. He felt betrayed that I would stall the delivery, *which in itself was anxiety provoking*, so that I could get some sleep. I didn't feel guilt for my choice, I was scared—scared to have a natural childbirth, and scared things might go wrong. I most likely delayed or stalled my contractions, I just wasn't conscious of it at the time. Admitting this is hard because I have held a

grudge against his behavior for years. I can see that I have a responsibili[t]
here too.

When the time came and I was fully dilated, I didn't push long and our
baby came into the world. They handed me a glistening baby girl. Her
eyes were the most beautiful gray moons I'd ever seen. I was numb, not
only from the epidural but raw fear. I was now holding our baby--the
baby that wasn't supposed to make it. Would she be ok to rest with me?
Will she live? My heart was wrapping her up and bringing her inside to b[e]
loved and held in a special place within me. My mind was racing and fear
was flowing. I was so scared to love our baby girl. I couldn't bear the
thought of losing her. I held on tight and stared at her big eyes and full
lips. The only thing we had for certain: this moment.

Driving home with our new baby, as I sat in the back seat next to Mae i[n]
her car seat, I was terrified. I was leaving the safety net of the hospital. I
had all the instructions, the warning signs to look for should something g[o]
wrong. *How was I to sleep? How was I to not worry every single second? How could [I]
leave her alone?* Something in me changed. I was spinning in a pool of fears.
I was paralyzed to discuss them with Adam; I wanted these fears to stay
because they helped me to feel. I was going between a numbed-out to
just-functioning state emotionally. To a state of: I can't move or do
anything because I am so afraid. My mind was trying to rationalize and
make sense out of everything we had experienced the last nine months.
Her physical body made everything real. I had 45 minutes in the car to sit
with this and get a handle on myself somehow. We were about to begin
living in a new way and being there was important.......

On the day of Mae's surgery to repair the chambers of her heart, we had
already overcome almost two years of growth and adjustments, and there
was still more to navigate. The night before was agony. Thankfully, I had
a surprise visit; she came by to kindly give me valium. I have no idea
where she got it—nor did I ask for it—she thought it might be a good
backup plan for me. Rebecca stayed with me and brought several laughs. I
wouldn't have known that I needed a distraction, but I was certainly

thankful for her visit. I never got to tell her how much that night meant to me. She passed away approximately two years later from COPD.

Looking back at how much we experienced—countless diagnoses, doctor visits, and conversations, watching over her while she slept, nervously shadowing her as she met her milestones—letting go of her hand this day was crushing. She was listless and sedated. I was the last to hold her, and she had her favorite stuffed dog with her. She was now 18 months old. Her eyes were so blue and full of promise. She has a light within that is blinding. We handed her back to God that day and prayed over her tiny body. Prayed that we were worthy of her return to us, that he still trusted us to care for her soul. Hours passed by and we were surrounded by friends and family. We each found ways to comfort ourselves during the minutes.

I felt like we were the stars of a silent film. No one spoke. We each sat there tapping, pacing, reading, journaling, eating. It was unsettling quiet, not peaceful early morning stillness. We were on pins and needles; the surgery was set to last eight hours. She was on a bypass machine, also known as life support. They had to repair the partition between the lower chambers of her heart. Once off the machine, she would be in NICU recovery for several days. As hard as the initial round of testing was before she was born, we were just beginning our march to her health and vitality. Up to this point, she had hit all the major milestones and at times we forgot that there was any type of issue with her heart. Her smiles were so bright and comforting that nothing else mattered.

We spent a week at Akron Children's Hospital in the NICU and stayed bedside every day. Adam and I took turns being with Mae and spending time with Alex. Adam's mother and father took Alex most of the time and visits with him were a nice break from the intensity inside the NICU. Other visits were from Nichol and her tuna casserole, (*it is the ONLY tuna casserole I will eat that is warm, with cheese. I'm pretty positive it would be world famous, if she would just share her secret ingredient!*). She also brought a stuffy for Mae named Lavender. It was a gift from her Mom, Michelle, and still has a place on her bed. Lavender is a treasured family friend. There's a dual reality that happens when friends or family come to visit the hospital, a way that we are used to interacting which is disrupted by the artificial atmosphere of the hospital rooms. Even though Mae was recovering wel[l] all of the beeps and chirps all day and night wear you down. There is no mental escape from your surroundings. I would look forward to the time[I] could scoot out of the room for a moment and step outside to the courtyard. This courtyard was a magical kingdom. It was where all of the parents gathered to breathe fresh air and commune. To look into anothe[r] adult's eyes and acknowledge: *I see your struggle. I am here. Somehow it will all be ok.*

 These strangers were a lifeline, a place of respite when none could be found. I wish we had exchanged numbers or a way to keep in touch. Sometimes it takes a decade to realize the gift one left in your heart. The acceptance I found there has helped me to accept circumstances that aren't the usual. Our daughter has had her own struggles from those early surgeries.

 During the time of Mae's healing, I received a call from Faith; she was unusually desperate and trying to beat around the bush. I politely reminded her that every one of my seconds mattered here and I didn't want to waste my time away from Mae to sidestep why she was really calling. She laid out a whole scenario about how her check didn't arrive and they are threatening to evict her. I asked where the money was that we had already sent her. What happened to her rainy day fund? Why is she calling her daughter that is in the NICU unit caring for her own daughter, to ask for money?! Was I really her last resource? I became furious. I needed a mother for once in my life! I needed her to ask me; "How are you, Brigid? How is Mae? Is there anything you might need from me?" Instead, it was the usual; take care of a phone call that I had received too many times to count. I was at my breaking point with her. Her health was also declining, and it was more than I could bear. I wasn't about to parent her, this time it was tough love.

 For once I am putting myself first, my need first. It was another hard day. I told Faith never to call me again. That as far as I was concerned my mother died, she was now dead to me. I slammed down the phone and laid my head in my hands and sobbed. Finally, all the quiet tears that had backed up all the way through my body were ready to come out. I didn't stop crying for hours. Snotty, sobbing, as Oprah calls it, "ugly crying." How can life be so beautiful and tragic in the same breath? Why is it hard to know where to meet people in their grief and hold their hands, when words no longer heal or help? I needed to be held with a grip that assured me my life would come back into some type of cohesive livable form. I needed to know that I could do this. I would rise and meet whatever the next step was in Mae's recovery, be there for Adam and Alex and still be a friend to myself. How would I know?

A few days later and we received the scariest news: Mae's heartbeat was consistently dropping below 50 bpm when she was resting. They rushed her down for testing to see what was going on with her. Adam and I were in shock. Everything was going so well. We thought for sure we would be discussing her discharge. Now we were back in the darkness of unknown. They concluded that her sinus rhythm was disrupted during the surgery and her heart was unable to keep a regular beat. They needed to take her back into surgery, put her on the bypass machine again and implant a pacemaker. This was the only option.

Adam and I rallied, we dug in deep within our trust of all we knew and believed in faith, family, and friends. We asked everyone to pray and please bring tuna casserole. It's a comfort food that goes right to the soul, through a tiny opening in the stomach, Nichol delivered!

Once the implant surgery was over, we were back in the NICU for an indeterminate time. Mae did very well during the surgery and seeing her wheeled back into the room was hope on a gurney. I use that word hope a lot and it's hard to know what hope looks like. Seeing your child breathing after a life and death surgery is hope. I will never know what it was like for her, having her heart beating through a machine and her blood suppressed so they could get to her heart. I imagine it's terrifying! Where did she place her faith and trust? Did she know she would be ok? That we were still there for her? Did she know that we were fighting for her to be here with us? These were only a small amount of the big questions I had. With no hope of receiving answers. How do you make a life and death choice for a child? Is it ever our choice to make? Were these obstacles in place so that we would all know how hard we could love and endure eve the most arduous circumstances?

The NICU was set up to provide the most comfort possible to the children and families who were staying for long periods of time. They ha a playroom for the children, brightly colored with various climbable Step 2 toys, a slide, books, and DVD's. Other areas were showers for the parents, a quiet room with fish tanks, another room for visitors and phone calls, and the outdoor area.

After weeks in the NICU, we finally received the news that we could go home!

As we left the hospital, I had mounds of paperwork, devices, and instructions. What no one could have prepared me for was her recovery. Something changed while we were in the hospital. Mae was still our blue-eyed, blondie. She didn't smile as often and she screamed every night. They called these night terrors. I don't know what it was, but it was horrific. Nothing would soothe her, she would scream and scream. The doctor said it might last for two weeks. We were back home, still feeling frightened. Going on two years of a steady state of heightened fear and anxiety, unaware at the time the toll it was taking on all of us. We were living in an elevated stressed state. I try to be gentle with myself when I look back.

There are many things I regret. Not being gentler, more patient, and kinder. Not trusting myself that I was the perfect person for her and our family, to manage these struggles. Forgetting that Adam was my right-hand partner, and shutting him out. I was too ashamed, exhausted, and sickened to let him see how much suffering I was in. I was terrified all the time. I felt slightly crazy, detached and distant. My coping mechanism was to not be fully present to what was happening. I was skimming the surface in our lives, trying to keep everyone alive for one more day. Making sure the children had what they needed. Putting on the outward appearance that everything was "fine." I really detest the word "fine." It's a copout to sharing what's really happening in my world. Because being vulnerable is too exposing, so I hid behind "fine." I didn't consider that I needed a break or someone to talk to about how I was feeling. We kept scooting along...

In my youth I was unfamiliar with what home was in the traditional sense. We moved often and lived in so many people's homes that I never considered the importance of one roof for a significant period of time. How the consistent presence of the shingles would help me begin to shed my own layers of pain. We moved into Nana's home once Adam finished graduate school at Kent State University. Alex was approximately 10 months and Mae was ripening in my belly. We knew that coming back to Cleveland would mean longer drives for our doctor's appointments, but we were both eager to return home and be closer to family and friends. I was feeling isolated with a young child, and another on the way. The days were long, and my bout of depression was deepening. I had postpartum depression after Alex, and they put me on Zoloft to help. It only helped a little. Where once there were endless tears, now I was numb, and detached from any interest in intimacy. My mental state was a constant dialogue of fear; which deepened when I was alone with my baby for countless hours a day. I was jealous of Adam's ability to come and go as he needed to. His days were full trying to provide income for us, while finishing his Master's degree. I used to tell myself unhealthy scenarios that he would fall in love with one of his students, because she would be interesting, able to carry on lengthy conversation, or at least had hobbies.

Clueless that I came programmed with an inner booklet that would help me to navigate all of the unknowns of mothering, I simply didn't believe I had any wherewithal to manage what seemed so natural to other mothers. I thought their wiring was attuned and mine was still frayed. Being back home would help me to have a few more eyes on my baby and me. I was desperate for more support. We lived with Adam's parents for a week or so and then moved into Nana's. She was elderly and needed more eyes on her. It seemed the perfect fit. I always enjoyed visiting her home when I was working nearby. We thought it would be a nice place for our children to call home for a time. Alex brought so much joy to her heart. I loved seeing her play with him and teach him. Her feet hurt her nonstop, but she managed to make her way down onto the floor to play with him for extended periods of time.

It isn't always easy navigating two generations under one roof. We both had ways of doing certain domestic chores that varied. I also didn't like being watched all of the time. The irony! I didn't like being alone, and I didn't like being with someone round the clock. Truthfully it was her home, and I never quite felt at home, similarly to when I was a child. I always knew to leave things as I found them because they didn't belong to me. Now I was doing that with a baby in toe. He touched and fussed with everything while he was learning about his world. I felt that I was constantly on edge to appease everyone around me. I wasn't appeased. I was spinning out of control, with worry, fear, and loneliness. I was deeply disconnected from myself. I didn't know the woman I was, or what I had to offer. I didn't even believe that I was fit to raise this bald human that followed me all day.

He was adorable. His full face had red cheeks and eyes as big as the moon. He was a quiet child, always watching us. He didn't say much, which left Nana always wondering when I would get him checked out. We had countless conversations about how "Children his age (10 months) are talking and vocal." This was her assumption, I found evidence to the contrary, but she was certain that something was wrong with him. Those statements triggered my guilt of overindulging with blue margaritas before I knew I was pregnant. Just great, more fuel for my "I'm not good enough to be a mother" arsenal. Light a match and I would implode.

After Mae was born, the tensions mounted. Alex, Mae, and I spent a lot of time walking. I would put him in the stroller, her in my papoose and we explored our neighborhood. It was a way for me to release the pressure I was putting myself under and to enjoy being with the children and nature. I didn't know it at the time, but I was learning to ground myself. During all of the miles I walked around outside, I was connecting to nature and calming my nervous system, which I needed more than I realized. The gift of home Nana was providing was exactly what Adam and I needed. I couldn't accept it at the time. She was grooming me to be a wife, trying to assist in my learning and maturing. We all know the story. The more an adult insists, the more they resist. I resisted.

We usually did not have a permanent residence, so we drifted from one experience to the next. This could be a rather exciting way to grow up— to be a gypsy of sorts—and I do have that in my blood. Perhaps it's residual from the way I was raised, or perhaps I came in wired that way. The circumstances, however, were not so colorful and cheery.

Faith was fighting demons that I've only recently come to understand. It was the year before her death that she was diagnosed with Bipolar Disorder. One day she called me on the phone; "Brigid, guess what?"

"Faith I don't know it could be just about anything."

"I have Bipolar Disorder!" She was excited, with a back note of relief— maybe this was an explanation for her of why things had been the way they were between us. I asked her what they were doing to help her. "I pop a few pills that will help me, and I'll be seeing a psychiatrist weekly. "

Finding out wasn't necessarily surprising, she was often an up and down person to me, it was the way she was, and I'd come to accept it. I noticed that she was finding acceptance in herself through the diagnosis. I took note of the diagnosis for myself and my children. It is something I will keep an eye on for each of us.

Some of her actions, the drinking, abuse of medications, even the various men that took her attention from me, I can forgive and accept, other pains are still surfacing. In the moments of her neglect and un-wellness, I was alone—left in situations with people, and in places, that no child should be left in. We lived in apartments that were infested with cockroaches. Many times home was an apartment of empty rooms, empty refrigerators, and no running water or utilities. We were homeless, with four walls around us. There were homes that were used as drug houses and puppy mills, homes that had elicit acts taking place. We lived in or stayed in hotels, where I would be locked in the room. These are all of the places I remember. I will assume that there's more I chose to forget. I was the victim of physical and sexual abuse, by men and women. Before the age of twelve, I had a very clear understanding of sex, drugs, and everything in between. I was my own daughter and mother to my mother. I was caring for her before I even knew how to care for myself.

Faith tried to keep an appearance of a well-groomed woman raising a child on her own. I went to private schools and lived in decent neighborhoods, but always on the outskirts of these areas. I'm still not sure how she afforded my education. Many times I remember being dropped off with dirty clothing and hair, and a wasted mom. She would be verbally warned by the nuns for her unacceptable behavior.

Once we drove up late, which wasn't uncommon. The nuns always waited outside of St. Philip and James school. As we tore around the corner, my door came unlatched and I literally rolled to a stop. Faith screaming, "Oh my God, Brigid! Shit! Are you okay?" The nuns rushing to dust me off and fluff me. The looks she received said everything. I scurried into school, humiliated at my arrival. I wasn't cool enough to pull off a stunt such as this. I was awkward in my steps, speech, and presentation.

The heart of a child is so pure that I idolized my mom for many years. She was my hero, the strongest person I had ever seen. She went through life with an unstoppable demeanor. The reality was that she was suffering. Her glossy exterior was not an accurate mirror of her internal war. I can see this now, maybe I saw it then too. I just didn't know how to make sense of it.

I have faint memories of her lining up and sorting through various shapes and colors of pills. She usually had an array, while my belly was growling. The indifference of priorities is what I find difficult to overcome. It's something that still comes into my daily life. I will have to weigh my conscience to see if it is ok to do something for myself or if my choice will take away from our children.

Another time we were at a stop light, it was dark. She was driving and rooting through her cigarette pouch. "Ah there it is," she said.

"There what is?" I asked.

"The blotter." She held up a little square, pinching it between her fingers.

"What is a blotter?" I asked.

"It's a psychedelic," she said with an excited chuckle. In her mouth it went, the light changed and we were back in motion.

I have heard people say that being physically abused may be worse than emotional abuse. After what I witnessed with Faith, who was a victim of both, I believe the emotional abuse is what broke her. I have never in my life witnessed such suffering in another human as I did in my stepfather. He was tormented, and we paid the price. He would routinely beat Faith, and she would be "laying down" or, worse, at the hospital because of the extremity of her wounds. Faith only had use of her left arm; it was harder for her to do certain things like drive a stick shift while smoking a cigarette or open jars, cans, etc. She always seemed "normal" to me, until someone would ask her what happened to her arm. She always came up with wild stories of it being bitten off by a shark or stuck in an elevator door and almost ripped off. The people who asked most likely wished they hadn't because what wasn't gruesome to look at, more of a curiosity, ended with a gruesome tale.

But James managed, through his tyranny, to convince my mother of her weaknesses. A woman that was my hero was degraded to a shell. Watching him break her was the hardest part of their relationship for me. Beginning in my sixth grade year in middle school until sophomore year in high school, we lived with him in a three bedroom apartment. I began working at twelve to help my mom with the bills. James sat home all day, drinking and planning how he would get rich. He had many schemes and Faith and I supported every one of them; the game room next to the bowling alley, rubber tire recycling, lamp shade making, and creating high end apartments along Lake Erie (which someone eventually did, to my knowledge it wasn't him).

As you can imagine, with the violence that I was exposed to, and routinely victimized by, it was hard to be present in the school, and even to show up some days was difficult. My heart was confused and scared most of the time. I didn't have a safe person. Faith couldn't keep me safe—she couldn't even protect herself! I couldn't keep her safe either. James made advances on me which she wouldn't believe, and I would feel his cold and piercing stare on my body often. I'm not sure which was worse to experience, his violation or Faith's denial.

It was a tough time in my development as a young woman. My body was changing and my thoughts on how I saw myself were changing. To feel his lust for me was disgusting. I didn't want to develop because I didn't want to be enticing in any way. I didn't want to be visible and thereby threatened. I tried to keep a low profile and do my daily chores. I can see now, looking back, that this is a key piece of my body images issues. I was rejecting a very natural and beautiful time in my growth. I was blossoming into my womanly body. At forty-two years of age, I still have moments when I look in the mirror and feel shame about being a woman. That by being my gender I am asking for some type of violation. I have had sexual dysfunction all of my post-puberty life. Being intimate is difficult for me, as well as being touched.

James used to stand over me when I was sleeping—run his fingers down my body. I woke to him fondling my breast and touching himself. To this day, I cannot be awoken in the night for intimacy without still seeing my step dad instead of Adam. Not welcoming Adam's affections after I've fallen asleep has created conflict in our marriage. All these years later, I still walk hunched over, shoulders curved, to protect my breasts. I've been hiding them ever since, because they are what James enjoyed.

I crave touch and connection, but trusting it is still painful. When my body was compromised things changed, I changed. I grew into someone who changed, while changing, and it never settled in quite right. Which leaves guilt, sadness, regret, and remorse, I feel for Adam who desires me as a beautiful woman, his partner, and wife. He craves intimacy and because of my traumas, I have a hard time delivering. For when I offer to touch it has a pressure of "more."

Sometimes I just want to experience touch without any morphing. I found freedom of touch without expectation, through an unexpected experience. My friend and spiritual partner Sarah was bringing the cuddling culture to Cleveland. In support of her, I offered to attend her second cuddle party. I had zero idea of what to expect, or what I was stepping into. The instructions were simple, come dressed comfortably, and you have full consent of how you spend your evening. Plan to be here for about four hours. Sounds easy enough. The party is set up in such a way that all of the ice-breakers and expectations are set in the safety of a circle, facilitated by the host. She went through many rules of cuddling, the dos and the don'ts. As I sat there my entire body seized. My legs felt like bricks and I had a hard time breathing. I knew that I was safe, there was no eminent danger, yet my body was responding to something I couldn't see!

Once the cuddling part of the party got underway, I summoned Sarah over and shared what I was experiencing. She held safe space for me to go inward and understand what was happening. My pain-body was activated. Because I have experienced non-consensual touch throughout my life, my body was seized in fear. Through breathing and holding the intensity, I felt the shift within my body AND I was able to participate. That evening I felt a part of something bigger than myself. I felt I was part of a family. Everyone who attended was kind, gentle and communicative. Each was there to share and grow, there was no pressure, no prodding. A lot of white space for me to find what I needed and to ask for it. The best part of the party was learning to say "NO" without any explanation. No was, in fact, a complete sentence.

As we moved about our lives in this haze of dysfunction and fear, I tried to maintain friendships and make connections. I had a few good friends during our Lakewood years; girls that felt safe and accepted me where I was. I wouldn't have people to our apartment because I couldn't trust James's actions. As I spent more time in other people's homes it became apparent just what we were dealing with in ours. No one else I knew lived this way. The ease and carefree nature my friends were afforded ate away at my heart. How I longed to be safe, seen, and loved in a way that people who aren't being abused can live.

I remember my middle school counselor—she was warm and inviting. I was sent to see her because of my poor attendance. I often attended school to escape, and as my peer group grew I would cut classes to stay at the pizza shop or walk around for a bit. I wouldn't open to her at first; for fear that Faith would be compromised. As the school year progressed, she and I developed a friendship. She had a daughter at the high school, and loved when she visited. I thought she was one of the coolest women I have ever seen. She danced into a room, with her long dreadlocks and unique clothing. Her confidence washed over me; her groundedness inside of her essence was enchanting. Her mother accepted her and celebrated her. I adored them both. It also stirred the feelings of disconnect I had with Faith. She was seldom with me, too busy licking her own wounds or trying to avoid new ones. How did she have time for me?

When I was in sixth grade I had a friend Angela who was African American. We got along really well, and I adored her. Angela and Kristen were two of the closest girls to me in Middle school. One day I took the step and invited her to our home. I was really excited for her to come over after school for lunch. She was hesitant but finally agreed. I was delighted that she said yes, though I didn't understand why she was hesitant.

The day finally arrived. We walked home after school and I prepared grilled cheese sandwiches when we got there. They were all I knew how to prepare well. As we sat and chatted, Faith came home. I called her to the back of the house to meet Angela. Faith came in and immediately lost her mind. She was screaming at her to "Get the F**k out of my house, you no good n***er!"

Over and over again she spewed slanderous comments. I stood there in shock, like a deer in the headlights, seconds before being run over! I couldn't for the life of me understand what was taking place. Angela flew out of my house in tears. I turned towards Faith and screamed at her. I kept yelling "Why did you do that?!"

She looked at me and said, quite sternly, "You are forbidden to bring another n***er into my home."

"What? How can you call her that? You don't even know her!"

"I've known my share and when you know one, you know them all," she said.

In my horror, I couldn't stop thinking about her and whether or not she made it home ok. Heartbroken at my mother's behavior, I knew that I had to see Angela. I barely slept that night, in anticipation of school the next day.

I walked to school earlier than usual and waited by her locker. She didn't show up. I went to first-period class, ever more anxious. *Maybe she stayed home? Maybe she dropped out of school? What if I never see her again?!* These along with numerous other scenarios played through my head.

Finally, lunchtime. We have been sitting with one another for at least a month now. I will surely see her at lunch if she is here today. When I entered the cafeteria, I saw her. My heart jumped and my eyes smiled. I ran over to her. She didn't even raise her head to acknowledge I was there.

"Angela, may I talk to you?"

"Go away!"

"Angela, I really need to explain."

"Get away from me."

"I will wait for you after school by the baseball diamond."

She said, "Oh, ok, great!"

"Thank you!! I can't wait to talk with you more. I am soo, sooo, soooooo, sorry."

She took her tray and left the table.

My gut sank, as I knew something was off. It's unlike her to not make eye contact. Sure, I knew her feelings are hurt, but there was a new side of her I've never seen before. I watched the clock for the next 90 minutes. Every tick, every tock, I waited, exploding anticipation. I just had to see her.

Ring, ring. The bell went off and we were free for the day. I ran to my locker, threw my books in and grabbed my coat. I ran down the hall and hopped steps to get outside as quickly as possible. As I approached the field, I saw a large group of kids hanging around in a circle. Hmmm, I wonder why they are all over here.

Then Angela stepped forward, her eyes were full of fire. She came charging at me.

"I hate you!" she screamed. The next thing I knew, I was on the ground being pummeled by her fists. She punched me over and over and over.

I was curled up in a ball, begging her to "Please stop. I am sorry. I didn' mean to... I didn't." More punishing punches.

All I could hear was my heart racing, the sound of her fists bouncing off of my body after each blow. Her breathing was so fast and growling. The crowd around us kept shouting "Fight, fight, fight!" "Get er, kick her ass!" "Fight, fight, fight!"

The punching stopped and I took a breath of relief, only to have it kicked out of me. Now she was on her feet and kicking me in my back. That pain sent chills down my spine. That was the last thing I can recall. When I came to, the crowd was walking away, and I was laying there in my own slobber and confusion.

I would never have imagined that my mother's choice would leave me in a puddle on the school grounds.

The ass beating of my life most likely lasted five minutes, but it felt like forever. My body hurt for days, my ego a lifetime, bruises everywhere. I can only imagine that each of my bruises was only visible signs of the bruises she received from my mother's words. How many times would she have to hear such gut-wrenching profanity shouted at her, for something that I found so beautiful? Her skin, hair, and eyes, were exotic and mysterious to me. She was different and I loved that about her. She also was the first friend I had that showed earnest interest in wanting to know me. We weren't friends because we were "popular", we were friends by choice. Two people looking to belong somewhere. She mattered to me, even after the fight. I still cared for her; I would pipe up anytime I heard another student talk about her.

She never spoke to me again. She left her mark by telling all of the students how my Faith was handicapped, with a "midget arm." The other students loved that gossip and soon made up little chants to taunt me with. I remember hearing adults talking about how kids can be cruel and relentless. I think the same of adults. Faith broke a girl's heart that day. What I had to bear seemed mild in comparison. The kids at my school eventually found a new kid to pick on and the attention moved away from me.

I wonder if she has forgiven me. That event hurts me still. I will forever be sorry for the pain that was inflicted by my naivety.

While I seldom invited people to our apartment, Faith and James would have card games, and their friends would be partying until the wee hours of the morning. I enjoyed some of their friends; the ones that would acknowledge me. About this time Uncle Tony moved in with us. I hadn't seen him for many years. He and my mom had a falling out around the time of my grandmother's passing. Oh, my grandmother. To hear stories of her today, she was a villain. To me, she was everything. I loved her more than I can remember loving anyone in my youth. She lit up when I entered the room; assured me I was the apple of her eyes. She lived in an assisted living residence with many colorful characters. The community they had there felt like Alice in Wonderland. Everyone was the brightest expression of themselves, and it was a play land for a young girl.

I would sit in the common room and listen to their stories and funny manners of speech. They would all delight in my visit, and I'm sure they added a few extra details to the delivery for my benefit. My grandmother was ailing and needed the help, but she seemed happy there. She was bound to a wheelchair and had mobility issues. I would often help her cook and clean while visiting. I have fond memories of those times. I would stay the weekend with her, and we would go the Schwebel's bread company up the street. The air always smelled of yeast and was delicious.

She gave me my first lessons in cooking. It was during one lesson that I learned the importance of NOT spilling bacon grease all over your feet. I was going to be Cinderella for Halloween and had such horrible blisters I couldn't wear my shoes!

Uncle Tony moving in with us at first added a layer of uncertainty. Looking back, I can see that he was a blessing. His presence when he was present was a pause for James's abusiveness. Uncle Tony would intervene before it got physical and protect my mother. He would also take me from the home and spend time with me.

One time he surprised me by taking me to a monster truck rally. I think every person should try one, once in their life. They are INSANE! The trucks are huge and they plow over cars. It was loud with rock music, smoky, and amped up! I loved every second of it. He was a car and truck enthusiast. Some Sundays he would take me to Brookside Park and we would go up and down the steep hills in his Ford F150. It would leave me with a dizzy, buzzy feeling. I balanced the line of being enthused and nauseated.

Uncle Tony had three children, but they moved out of state with his ex-wife after their divorce. When he was married I remember going to their home for Easter. Uncle Tony, being the jokester that he was, would have a bunch of dyed chicks running around in a pen in his backyard! They would always bring delight to us children, and we found it loads of fun to chase them. I guess the divorce was difficult, and they deemed her to be the best parent to my cousins. Maybe I was helping him to heal, as he was helping me to feel safe in a man's company...

As the years moved on we became good friends with others who lived in the apartment complex. My mother became best friends with Sunny, and she had five children. Some were close in age to me. Next door was Deb, who had two children, and I had a huge crush on her son, Joe. Our upstairs neighbors Anne and Sal also became friends. I didn't realize they would be more angels to me. We finally had a community that we belonged to. I really enjoyed playing with kids my age, and settling into school, making friendships, and being a somewhat typical kid. I could finally exhale, and not be the one caring for Faith all the time. Even though I began working at a young age, that role seemed to alleviate some of my motherly roles.

Sal and Anne lived above us with their son Tim. We were about the same age; he was a nice boy, with a soft heart and quick wit. He could make me laugh through the toughest of times. He kept me on my toes because he was the first person I met with a pacemaker. Back at that time, you would have to advise anyone with a pacemaker to step out of the room if a microwave was turned on. It would interfere with the device and could be problematic. Tim used to kid with me that the microwave was turned on and he would convulse like he was dying. It was a real hoot—NOT! I like to kid with those closest to me that I dye my hair dark because I am a blonde at heart. Now, I am not knocking blondes. I am comparing myself to the silly blonde jokes that I grew up hearing in the 80's. I secretly believe that brunettes are the originator of all the ill-meaning blonde jokes, it was their way of invoking revenge at all of the fun the blondes were having! We brunettes tend to take ourselves too seriously. Tim's parents befriended Faith and although they didn't hang out often, like some of Faith's other friends, they did know what was happening in our lives and paid close attention.

Tim and I would hang out with a few of the other kids in the area. I mostly bummed around with boys that were roughly 2-3 years older than me. Most of them I considered good looking, and they were chummy. None had an interest in me that I knew of, or noticed. It made it easy to be like one of the boys. This persona helped me stay under the radar. I already wanted to be invisible to the opposite sex. The more I developed physically, the greater was my desire to not be seen. I didn't like the way James's eyes followed the blossoming curves of my body. I was thankful for the door lock on the inside of my room. Why it was there I am still not sure. Faith installed one on both sides of the door. I could use mine when I needed and so could she. This was a habit that began long ago when we lived in hotels. I would be locked in the room, to ensure my safety. It wouldn't be until my adult years that those scars would begin to seep their toxins.

Being locked in small rooms created a great deal of anxiety inside of my body and mainly my psyche. This was something that I suppressed and when it rose, was unexpectedly troublesome.

Sal and Anne were both large personalities. Sal was a robust man, who spoke loudly, with grand hand gestures to follow his vocal chorus. He was a great conductor of his own symphony. Anne was more reserved until she was comfortable and then she too was quite boisterous. She loved Tim very much. I could tell by the way she would involve him in conversations and encourage him to participate in making decisions. They weren't a nuclear family, (from what I gathered, Sal was Anne's partner, not Tim's biological Dad) but they were a family. I envied any of my friends that had a family atmosphere in their home. I could never reconcile why they had that and I didn't. I wondered why it was that no matter who Faith fell in love with, none of them felt like home. Our home wasn't ever calm and predictable. It was predominately erratic with lots of arguing, coming and going, and partying.

Anne raised and bred the most beautiful gray and yellow Cockatiels. Faith decided it would be a great idea to buy a bird from Anne. I enjoyed being around birds from my stay with Bertha, and had a pet Parakeet, name Petey when we moved into W.117th. He was a parting gift from Bertha. Faith's Cockatiel lived with us for one day. After Anne went to great lengths of trimming his feathers and taught Faith basic care tips, someone was coming in the back door of the apartment and out went the bird. She chased him for a stint and to our surprise he could fly just high enough to escape her capture!

Anne and Sal had a bird's eye view of our life. They could hear everything through the walls and floors. Sal never liked James and didn't make any pretense that they would be friends or that he was ok with the way James treated Faith. After our first year in the apartment, Sal made it known to James that he wouldn't turn a blind eye to the abuse that was taking place. By our third year, the tensions were mounting. James kept promising he would give up drinking and give Faith and me the life we deserved. How could he possibly know what that looked like? I never knew what we deserved. By this point I was accepting what he offered as usual behavior. I knew it wasn't normal, yet, it was my normal. It was also tearing me apart inside. I was in deep depression, although it was never spoken of in that way. I was labeled as "troubled." Guess what: when you grow up with addicts all around you, you become some form of troubled as a coping skill. At this time I was having chronic lower back pain. It was excruciating at times and I would stay home from school for days, sometimes weeks. The truancy officer began getting to know me.

Faith always blew it off, and assumed that her passivity would help whatever was ailing me. She took me too many doctors, all of whom told her I was faking. There was nothing physically wrong with me, it was all psychological. That's when I met the man with the ink blobs. He had no idea how to get inside my locked up world. I would sit there for an hour each time and he would show me strange images on cards and ask me to tell him what I thought they were. I had no idea what they were; they were purposely distorted and didn't look like anything I could recall. I balked at this attempt to help me. No one ever asked me what was going on in our home. It was always surface level questions, nothing that would break a seal of my secrecy. I knew by this time to keep my mouth shut about Faith's drinking and pills and about the people who had sexually abused me. No one wanted to hear about my trifles. I was an average girl, having an average experience, at an average time in my life.

Doesn't everyone go through rough patches? Isn't it normal to live in an apartment with little food and intermittent utilities, with roaches running around everywhere? It was the norm from where I was coming from. I remember the first time James touched me. I woke to him fondling my breasts and touching himself. I startled him by jumping up with disgust. He hurried off as quickly as the roaches when the light switch is flipped.

The next morning, I told Faith what had happened and she blankly looked at me and said I was lying. I felt utterly defeated, powerless, and alone. *Goddamnit! When will someone believe me?* These nighttime visits continued, and my only choice was to pretend I was asleep and didn't notice. Since Faith didn't believe me, I had no one else to protect me. I never had any sense of control or power the entire time they were married. I was the ghost that was noticed when they needed something, the ghost that provided a paycheck and kept fairly quiet.

As James's tyranny worked its way through our psyches and sense of worth, he finally hit the grand finale. That night he and Faith went out. He came home; she was rushed to the ER. I never did find out the whole truth. When I saw her, she was broken. Her spirit lost its shimmer. No matter how bad things had been up to that point, she always glowed. It was part of her magic. It was as if the tiny bits of hope she held onto made her skin and eyes shine. After the physical assault, she was dulled. I can't say that I blame her, but I did. I blamed her for everything. I blamed her for falling into his traps. I blamed her for not putting me first. I blamed her for being weak. I blamed her for believing in him more than her. I blamed her for never leaving. I blamed her for not believing me. I blamed her for putting us both at risk, every fucking day! Every day! He broke many bones in her face, her arm, her heart, and her spirit. He broke us. The day I walked in to find her on her hands and knees begging him not to leave her, after almost killing her, broke us. I never saw Faith the same. I could barely look at her, partly because I was scared to death that she may not recover. Also, I hated that I couldn't protect her. I couldn't keep him away from me, how was I supposed to keep her safe? His eyes were always beady, piercing one's goodness. His heart was closed and he took everything he could.

James: 2, us: 0. Victory.

While Faith was in the hospital, I was going to school and work. I was so glad to have a means of being away from the house. I came home early one evening and found our front door wide open. It was strange, out of place, and I proceeded with caution. As I stepped into the apartment, things were thrashed about. There was blood all over the wall and a large amount of fecal matter strewn down the hallway. James was nowhere to be seen. I made my way all to the back of the apartment and no one was home. As I walked back to the front, I was met by Sal. He told me that he gave James what was coming to him. He paid him back for all that he had done to Faith.

My body trembled as my mind was trying to escape into a daydream. This was all so much to take in. I couldn't believe the courage that he displayed in my mother's honor. The police were involved and investigated what took place between Sal and James. There weren't any witnesses and Sal claimed it was self-defense. I will never forget the gift he gave us.

Within a week or so, James moved out when Faith and I weren't home. When we returned, we found that he cleaned out our entire apartment. He literally took everything. That was his way to suck people dry and move to a new town, begin again. When Faith met him, he was being pursued by the Michigan police for outstanding child support. He had several children that he didn't take care of. Faith was an easy target for his domineering, manipulative ways.

I have spent many years trying to understand why things happened the way they did. I have worked through forgiveness countless times towards James. There are some things I will never understand, and I am uncertain that I will ever fully forgive him. I know that inside of the man we lived with there is a young boy, who most likely never learned to have his needs met with care and nurturing. He didn't know how to love my mother. She didn't know she deserved love. They were magnets in their suffering. I was the witness. I still struggle to this day with being defensive, protective and closed off. It is very hard for me to keep my heart open. To know that I am safe. That my body will not be violated. It is a constant effort on my part to heal. Let go. Begin again.

For My Mother
Unhinge the cage of your rage
What he called love
Began with a shove
Subtle
An accident
Did the canary know as she peered through the window
All she had given away
I wondered as I watched her confused
Blank
Sullen
Expression
It happened in less than an hour
He exuded what he called power
Known as might
Not with wisdom
Charisma
Restraint or
Charm
He held her by her arms
Brutalized her from the outside in
Not a chance for her to win
Fucking coward!
Riotously
Silent
Trembling
Watching the horror
I was helpless
Abhorrent
The hero I looked up to
Now a caged canary
No longer yellow
Covered in black and blue
Taking her bravery
And choking her with it
So much courage she had

To surrender
In the pain of his hands
Taking it over and over
Giving away more than he ever knew
Too scared in himself
To look at her bruises
Scuttling around, head hanging down
Wished he'd packed up and moved to a new town
He waited until his next drink could be found
Courage in a bottle is what they called it
I saw it as a rat detector
More alluring than cheese
Bringing a grown woman to her knees with brutality
No humanity
Fucking coward!
As I stare out the window replaying that day
I watched her flutter about
Silently searching the winds
For the only thing, she had left
Her voice....
Latent
Unheard
She thought it absurd
Being silenced
And began to sing
Anywhere, to anyone
Her time of oppression
Has ended
Jubilee suspended
Never being small
Beyond his might
She started a new
Living as best she could
Protecting what mattered most
Ignoring the pains of the ghost
As she was someone's hero

Beginning with the beats in her chest
Reflection in the mirror
She had nothing more to fear
Sing Canary Sing
It's the first day of spring!

After James left, we returned to the manic cycle of existing. I was growing, and able to do more babysitting after my job at the Brokerage Firm. Uncle Tony was helping us financially, and Faith was hitting the pills harder than ever. Though we were all earning a wage, and pooling it toward our survival, we routinely had one of our utilities disconnected. It made getting ready for school and work a challenge. I got used to it and carried on as usual. I gained a certain resolve around uncertainty - an acceptance almost. I could tolerate the lack of utilities because for once there wasn't constant screaming. In our later years, we moved further into Lakewood and stayed in a one and a half bedroom apartment. It had a murphy bed that would pull out of the wall in the living room. While Faith slowed on her drinking and pills, I took over her stead and was beginning my own manic cycle of abusing substances to distance myself from my pains

I call this my dream. My memories are fragmented and somewhat distorted. This dream is something that still interrupts my life. I first started seeing glimpses of memories when I was in therapy. She told me I repressed it; I am still keeping it at bay. I didn't want to go all the way in. It holds me back from achieving the life I most desire because I feel that I am soiled and tainted. Not wishing to be seen, known or desirable to the opposite sex. That's my inner child's wish. I, as a grown woman, have different desires and agenda.

When times were tougher than usual, we moved in with a friend of Faith's. I was told to call him "Uncle Cole." His house was a large two-story home with a nice front porch facing a quiet neighborhood.

Inside the walls, it was a poisonous place for a child. Faith was deep in her addictions and I was there to witness the fantasies being played out by the adults. It looked like a home, but it was a drug house. The door opened and closed too many times a day to count. I seldom knew anyone that was coming in and out. When the door was latched tight I could finally breathe.

In the basement lived the other feral animals. Uncle Cole had a girlfriend who would repeatedly tell the story of how he tried to kill her by shooting her point blank in the head. The bullet went straight through and left her with only minor damage to her brain and skull! She had slurry speech, interrupted memory, and a gentle, fearful smile.

The only difference between the four-legged animals and the two legged were the metal bars. The animals were in some ways safer, removed, and forgotten. They were eager to receive affection and attention. This place caused me great anxiety. Bobo recently died, Faith was drowning in her grief. Still feeling lonely and in jeopardy most of my days, I did get relief from going to school, though I wasn't a model student. I often wished the school days would stretch longer, only so that I didn't have to go back to the house with no soul. I adored the street, and some of the friendships I was beginning to make. I used to make mud pies with a girl down the street, Christina. She was always upbeat and interested in playing. She didn't go to the same school as me. Weekends were a great time for us to be child-like. I didn't have an easy time trying to connect with other children. I often felt like the oddball. Playing didn't come naturally to me; nothing about games was intuitive to me either, and I had to be shown all of the rules multiple times in order to participate.

Uncle Cole's house was a black hole that would inevitably pull me back into its density. I would often hide in my room, as it had a lock on the door. The lock gave me a sense of security when Faith was away, which was often. I can remember this man. When he entered the house I had chills dancing up my arms and the nape of my neck. The sight of him sent off every alarm bell my body could muster. He was large, heavy in body, I knew that he wasn't a good man—his eyes, his walk, the way he smelled—it all wreaked of malintent.

It was this man that got through the lock and made his way onto the edge of my bed. He softened his voice and spoke in a whisper. Trying to ease me, as if it would bring me comfort now that he is on the other side of the lock. It was late at night and the house was quieting down. I could still faintly hear the hum of the record player. My cat mittens hissed and swiped at this man, he smelled his ill thoughts. The fear that was coursing through me kept me from looking directly at this man. I knew that when he left, I would never be the same again. It was if all of my senses went off line. I didn't feel the full weight of his heaviness, his scent, and any sounds he made. I watched as my small body was pressed against his. I was above us, removed from the physical discomfort. I couldn't be a part of his attack. I was consoling myself from afar.

After that night I began having fainting spells. I would be walking or talking and completely black out. The most egregious part of that man's taking was my sense of safety, which was already scantily available. Having no place to call home within my own body destroyed my inner structure.

There was an ambulance that night. I was bleeding and I assume Faith called them to get me help, or find out what had happened. I do not remember if I told her, I only remember seeing bloody panties and an ambulance. She never spoke of this night directly to me. I retreated into the deepest corners of myself and began dimming my light. I wanted to disappear and become a ghost amongst the waken.

The ambulance came to the house a few times. I would wake up to an EMT standing over me, yet somehow Uncle Cole was never arrested for selling cocaine and allowing abusers into his home. To this day I still do not recall all of the details. My brain protected me, and my spirit survived. The fainting stopped when I moved in with Bertha.

I keep unraveling this mystery one painful thread at a time. I may never reach its end, I may not need to. One can only relive a trauma so many times before it begins to create more harm than healing.

The memories of that night started resurfacing about two years ago when I attended the cuddle party, when we were going through all of the rules, and how important consent is. Just hearing that word—consent—I began to freeze. I could no longer be present to the group. I was deep inside of my own pain. The pain I had ignored most of my life.

The man who stole my innocence may not even be alive any longer. I have suffered long enough from his deed. Through my own inner work, I have come to learn that I am not tainted or unworthy because someone abused me. I deserve to forgive myself for not being able to defend myself. I deserve to forgive myself for leaving my body and suppressing the enormous pain that was inflicted. To allow that night to remain a dream. I do not see the value in trying to live each step of that night over in my body. We have suffered long enough. I hold my hand to my inner child and I tell her….

There is a girl. Her hair in gnarled curls. She doesn't worry about how she looks. Life is too intense to turn away for such trifles as appearance and vanity. Undesiring of being pleasing to the eye of men. She lives her life afraid and scared. Living in the shallows of my heart. How did this relationship come to be, a disowned part of me? This girl loves me, with all her might. She will claw, scratch and fight for my safety. I look away, too ashamed to accept her valor. Why am I the one externally representing our dignity? She is so much stronger than me. When life becomes scary, I turn into mush, tremble and weary. The girl keeps her eyes open, recording every detail, noting our existence. I keep trying to float above, dropping in now and then to say hello my dear friend. I see you, I know you are tirelessly defending a place so tender and dear, I avert my eyes at the purity.

I am tainted and shameful. Tossed around like a ragdoll by the whims of "them", men, women, strangers, even family. All took pieces of us that I couldn't protect or defend. They ripped away our innocence, safety, self-respect, our voice. Unaware that as a child I had the choice to say NO, I didn't know that I had willpower or defenses. I left us; I left you, to fend off their advances. I wasn't as brave as you. I didn't know what else to do, I left.

I hate myself for doing this to you, us. I hate that I gave up the trust you once placed in me. Do I even deserve amnesty? This is why I hide from you. I feel shame, sadness, and remorse. I do not know how to stay the course with such intense disdain for my own self. I release and release, and release, and release. How can I ever take the taint of those hands on my skin and find peace within? I was betrayed by the people sworn to protect me. They were the ones that left me with blood stained panties. How can I forgive myself, me, you, and them? I do not respect myself, or those men and women. I felt their suffering, disease, and contempt. They loathed their own vile skin and slithered away like a stone man. How can I forgive the heinous acts that stripped the bark of my innocence, love, and respect? For me, not for them. I've searched, prayed, pleaded, slept, wept, cried, wailed, sailed, and nailed myself to my own cross of damnation. When will this hole of pain be filled in? What does it take? I understand. I am sorry. I plead to be released from this sorrow. It ruins my tomorrow's ray of warmth and acceptance. My divinity stands on the other side of this gully. Consistent in offering me salvation. I dare to step in that direction, for my shame and condemnation block my own desire to live a life of joy.

I turn to the girl and say, will you show me the way? How to love, live and forgive? We deserve a life of authenticity, freedom, and joy. Not to hide or wallow in the shallows of our own misguided ploys. I love you. I need you. You are everything to me and this is why I skirt around, flutter about. I do not know how to love this fiercely and have no doubts. It scares me to be this vulnerable, open and attached. I give this to you my inner Brigid, scaredy cat. You are the world and I am here. To take in the views, as you choose the pace, direction, and expression. We work as one.

There is a difference in being victimized and being a victim, admittedly it is hard to tell the difference in the midst of any trauma or intensity! One helps, one hinders. I was victimized in my life, sexually, and emotionally. And, I have had bouts of feeling like a victim. I have even benefited from this belief during some parts of my life. I used my victim to survive, to feel that I mattered, by making villains out of others to compare in some way that I was better than or at least not as bad off as they. What I continue to work on in my life is learning how to unhook from the events that happened to me as situations I couldn't control, I didn't ask for or deserve.

Now I know this is pretty radical. I did gain something. Not when I was younger, I was most certainly affected negatively. I made a lot of agreements of why these things happened to me. That it was my fault. People stole my innocence, or that my good nature drew people to me. I have hidden from the world in different ways. I'm still a good hider. I didn't apply myself in school, even though I know that I am smart, without trying hard very hard. It's a gift of my DNA. I didn't want to admit that I was smart and, not living up to my potential; I skipped school and flunked out. It never felt good to show up after missing day after day because I was too busy getting high or hanging out to attend school. I was above it. I was also trying to stay out of our house. Times were difficult, and I was always trying to make sense of the senseless.

My inner world disheveled and no amount of logic or effort was going to change my circumstances during those years. Faith still had a lot of influence over my care. Only when I was at school did I feel I had a sense of control over my choices. By this time I had already learned to not respect myself very much.

I had been in a sexually and mentally abusive relationship with a girl that was Faith's friend's daughter. Though I didn't consider it abusive at the time, I found it confusing, and dirty. I didn't know of the word abuse. I thought I had done something to initiate her advances. In my later years I used these early events to try and get a male's attention, as I noticed that to boys it was cool for two girls to be together. That too felt gross, and I was trying on different stories to see which one would get me noticed. I can own my part in benefitting in some way from the events that took place between us.

She took a liking to me which lasted for roughly five years. She liked to "play" with me, mostly my vagina, breasts, and mind. She left her mark inside of my developing sexuality and psyche. Faith was too busy to notice and thought she was doing me a favor by leaving me with the older girl (by four years) to look after me on the weekends. All of our years together weren't bad. I'm only putting emphasis on the abuse to anchor my latter point. Being the daughter of an addict with self-worth issues isn't a fun way to rise up in the world. I have a ton of fear of being known, YET, and this is a big YET. I also, have insatiable burning within to be out in the world. I am in constant battle with myself to work through what is real, or true. I absorbed a lot of Faith's distortions of what a woman is, what gives her worth, and what role she plays in the world. I have never felt comfortable being domestic or partnered.

Thinking of myself more as a wild horse that is meant to roam the plains, to forage for her sustenance. I learned that when I am given something it seldom came without condition. While being a self-sufficient entity was a principle I highly valued, being conditional nullified my authenticity. I can now see that my thinking was self-protective and limiting. While I believe in being able to care for myself, I have also discovered the most about my inner world by being a mother, and a wife, and a friend.

There is so much that life throws our way. Not everyone experiences trauma, but they do experience struggle. It is my life mission to help the pain be known and transformed. I believe that pain is a great teacher. It isn't cement! It is something we move through to polish more of our golden edges. Without pain, there's little catalyst for exploration or change. It makes people do something different, even if the different moves in a downward spiral, it is still movement. There is no path to wholeness by exclusion. Everything in our lives holds purpose. EVERY damn thing. It's a disservice to the difficulty to not use it as leverage to come unstuck.

Throughout all of this chaos, there were always people who I can now see as my angels; people who understood on a broader level the actual state of my affairs. They were sent to me to help alleviate some of the hardships I was facing. My mother was a master weaver of enticing good people to us. She used them to benefit her agenda. I was always embarrassed by that behavior and wondered why anyone would be manipulated. Was I also a part of this plot? I was part of the trap! It disgusts me to think of this, but I can't accept blame as I was too young to really know what was happening, but something always felt "off."

People stepped in because they could see that I needed a breeze of love, safety, and contentment. No matter how short-lived, it was felt and much appreciated. There were many neighbors, or friends from work who took us in when we were evicted, which happened frequently. There were teachers at many of the schools I "visited" —I didn't stay enrolled at one school until sixth grade. Some of the people who helped were struggling as well, but deep inside they had compassion for me. A level of care that I wish they had given to themselves, but I happily took it, because I needed to be held, too. I really started making connections when I was in sixth grade. That is the time that we stopped moving around (not that things were better). My mom had married and moved in with an abusive alcoholic. When she wasn't joining him in drinking, she was using pills and smoking marijuana, I was passed a joint more times by Faith and James, then any of my friends. Their volatile relationship was my nightmare. I am thankful that we stopped moving long enough for me to begin making friendships. It takes practice being a friend. Letting people get to know me was difficult.

Chapter Four
Learning a New Way

Before I knew of chakras, crystals, or healing work, I knew sadness, pain, and loneliness intimately. In order to check out from those dark places, I drank, ate, smoked, and looked away. The trouble was, it only made those places within angrier and more intense. My inner world was desperately trying to get my attention. It began with depression. It should more accurately be termed: Disconnection. That was the state of my life: disconnected from feeling anything I had buried within.

I was standing in Nichol's kitchen, Zoloft in my right hand, water in my left. I felt completely defeated. I wasn't "strong" enough to beat depression and now I am taking this damned pill that I swore I'd never take. My therapist suggested I try it, since two months of therapy yielded no improvement. My midwife referred me to her after they diagnosed me with postpartum depression. I think this depression has lived with me most of my life. I call it many names; lonely, sadness, fright, unlovable, invisible.

Standing there, I wondered if I was forever destined to be sad. Maybe I am not a person who deserves love and happiness; maybe I wouldn't know what to do with it anyway. She listened, I rambled. All of these thoughts needed a place to land. No action, no soothing, just to be let out. I needed to make room for the pill to go down.

Taking the pill turned out to be easier than the side effects. Those warnings they put on the white sheets inside of the box seem implausible. I mean why would anyone take a pill that can do so many harmful things?! Zoloft often made me numb. I felt little fluctuations in my mood and nothing below my belt line. I already struggled with this from my earlier experiences.

Sex never seemed to bring ease to my body. Being married and in a long term relationship didn't help the tension to disappear. It wasn't an error of Adam's; it was years of feeling afraid to be touched or naked with another. The Zoloft kept everything numb and my interest went from waning to none. I added this symptom to my running lists of things that were wrong with me and reasons to beat myself up. Not that I needed more reasons, my inner bully had free reign at this season of my life. Wasn't the whole point of taking these pills to help me not feel bad about myself?

My gaze rested on the small brown and white speckled tiles. I gasped and took in a deep breath, remembering a time when things didn't feel beautiful or possible. Life is beautiful, so beautiful in fact it overwhelms my senses. I feel the steady stream of tears fall as I move slowly, directing my next breath. Everything is in harmony. Just as the sun orbits the moon, all of life has cycles. As each day's cycle completes, old pain, patterns, and thoughts may fall away, creating room for new possibilities that dawn with the sun's rise.

Thirteen years ago I left a handwritten letter on our kitchen table. The table sits in the same kitchen as the speckled tiles. I wrote a letter asking Adam, our son, and family to forgive me. *Please forgive my choice to end my life. I cannot go on another day with the pain that weighs down my heart. You will all be better without me.* Those thoughts were so constant and strong that I believed them. I believed I no longer had anything to offer, no one would miss my absence. Life was spinning more quickly than I could hang on. Our life was in crisis; I was overwhelmed, exhausted, and felt utterly alone. Having someone to care for doesn't take away the lonely.

I walked outside, lit a cigarette and looked up at the sky as I sobbed and begged and pleaded for one more breath of hope. Instead, pulling toxicity and cloudiness into my lungs, there was no more hope to be found. My belly full of the life of our unborn child. Would the baby forgive me? After all we have been through, would she understand that her fate would not be fulfilled? I would not be here to deliver her, only carry her life a few short months before taking both of ours. I had my pocket filled with pills from the medicine cabinet; aspirin, Motrin, sleep aids. I knew that if I took enough of them I would fall asleep. Numb on the inside, cold on the out. The stars were brilliant, the air crisp, clear.

I stamped out my cigarette and exhaled the bitterness. My breath was filled with tar, nicotine, regret. I began to walk into our backyard when the side door opened. I looked back, surprised, as everyone was sound asleep. It was Alex, he was 13 months old.

"Momma?" he said.

"Yes, honey, I am here."

"Momma, I'm scared." *Me too honey*, I thought. He put out his hands for me to hold him.

"Yes, Alex, I will be right there." As I walked into the house I scooped the letter into my hand and crumpled it up.

There was one last breath of hope, it was muddled and found. Just as muddy as my thoughts all those years ago. I used to feel immense shame over that night. *How could someone like me even consider such an act!* I judged myself so harshly for my desperation. I was desperate for the intensity in my life to lessen, to be released from feeling inept and unable to cope. A few months later I told Nichol the story about this night. "Why didn't you call me?" she asked. I couldn't, I didn't know what to say or how to ask for help. It felt easier to end my life, then ask you or Adam for help.

Who Am I?

I could say it all began with that question. The reality is that I didn't know who I was. I was running through my life blind. The only sight I had was to be approved of. Everything I did was a means to be kept safe, to mean something. I never felt I belonged to anyone or anything. I had a deeper feeling of being invisible, so I worked really hard to be seen, known, and loved. This was a blessing in the early part of any relationship, which in the later years (if I got that far) would end up being a big hole of pain, leaving one to wonder how the woman who once loved them so much now pretends they're not even there. These were all strategies. I learned that if people really like having me around, I could eat for another day and have shelter. If they liked me too much, I didn't have the capacity to be vulnerable and stay connected. Once anything became too familiar or close, I needed an exit plan.

Faith was a masterful teacher of this strategy, I always watched with admiration for its efficacy. How ironic I never felt like one of the shiny things she loved to lavish her affections towards.

Time has a way of softening us, letting our eyes open to a wider aperture. Much of who I am today was from the early influences in my life. We all have tactics to keep us alive. Where I once held disgust, I now look at these qualities with compassion. I needed to survive to be here now, raising three remarkable children in a world of turmoil and uncertainty. Maybe all generations face this, I'm not sure. I never wanted their struggles to look like the ones I grew up in. I knew that I could give them the comfort of not having an addict for a mother that I would tell them every day how much I loved them, what they mean to me. While I held true to most of my promises, it turns out I do have addictions, my most predominate is to my suffering. My pain was a familiar nest to rest, comforting. I have spent a great deal of my life with Adam and our children living from a place of shadows and regret. Though I didn't know this at the time, the awareness has come from the deep work of being 100% accountable for who I am. I've moved farther away from being a survivor and having the strong desire to thrive in this world, even with the chaotic upheavals we are currently facing (climate change, pollution to our water and air, human trafficking, animal extinction, corrupt leadership, etc..) Finding a consistent pathway where I can connect with peace, contentment, and happiness is important to me. I find that it may, in fact, be one of the greatest pieces of my childhood that left too soon.

I embarked on a journey that wasn't romantic, inspired, or exotic. It felt like I dropped down an elevator shaft without any warning that the elevator was on the bottom floor. I had a long and bumpy freefall.

I've affectionately termed my experience The Big Quiet.

It began with a series of panic attacks. Looking back, I can see they were an invitation to do something with myself—other than depend on others for my daily dose of survival and safety. That's right: I was codependent. Being a stay at home wife and mother the last 15 years ma have been the catalyst, but truthfully, this was in me from my youth. Growing up with Faith, I learned many strategies to stay alive.

I was driving to the mall, listening to music, when suddenly I became disoriented, dizzy, short of breath, and terribly clammy. I pulled off the highway and phoned Adam. He said he'd be right there. I lay down on th side of the road gasping for air because I didn't want to die in my car! Confident I'd never see my children again, I wondered if they knew how much I loved them. Did I give them a proper goodbye? How many more things I wished to show them, say to them.

There I lay with a wildly rapid heartbeat, regret coursing through my veins. A police officer arrived before Adam; he asked to call an ambulance. I assured him my husband was en route and I would be ok. Adam arrived moments later with the kids. They loaded me in the car and as we drove farther away from the spot I began to feel slightly better. I came home, rested, hydrated and chalked everything up to not drinking enough water after our being at a Fourth of July party the night before. I dismissed what had happened and moved about in my dream.

A few weeks later we were all packed into the car, headed out for a day at the beach. As I drove, I began having the same feelings as before. I pulled over and didn't have the time or attention to soothe the worried looks on everyone's faces. I jumped out of the car and prayed hard. I prayed to never feel this way again, and this time I went to the hospital. We found the nearest ER to our location; Adam drove me there, and kept telling the children everything will be ok. *How did he know?* I wondered. *How was he so certain everything would be ok?* As we arrived, they put me into a wheelchair and rushed me into the back. I remember squeezing our children so hard I could hear their breath leave them. With tears in my eyes, I was in the unknown.

They ran tests (EKG, echocardiogram, blood work, monitors), everything came back negative for heart problems. Hours later I was discharged as having a panic attack. The doctor suggested I see my primary care physician. A few days later I went in. He ordered more tests, an MRI, another EKG, and Cardiac Sonography, but everything came back normal. I followed up with my primary care physician, he spoke with me about my options; therapy, medication, stress reduction.

I refused anti-anxiety medication after my experience with Zoloft for postpartum depression and instead I opted for therapy. The panic attacks kept coming, and so did my level of instability. I soon began to feel unsafe in my body. Not knowing when a panic attack would strike. They often left me feeling very depleted and defeated. It was hard to leave my home to make it to my therapy sessions, drive to work, or drop off our three children at school. All of my daily routines were now in question and falling to the wayside. Our home began to collect dust and dirt, our gardens abandoned; the way of life I knew couldn't exist in the way I knew it. I now lived with a looming feeling of uncertainty. I no longer trusted anything I once depended on.

Everyone I knew was supportive and kind as they could be, they seemed to understand that I wasn't myself, and I think quietly they had hoped things would return to normal. That's the problem; I didn't want support. I wanted to hide, run, never to be seen this vulnerable again. I felt like a loser, and terribly ashamed of my new level of unpredictability. Everything was in a state of flux; anything I once clung to for my sense of security could not bring the same comforts. Anything that comforted me was external and no longer worked.

NO amount of help, consideration, or understanding was going to change what I needed to do, which was to live through this new level of discomfort. Up until my first panic attack, I was cruising through major life events in a functioning way. I felt but didn't deal with any of the emotions that accompany death, birth, job loss, relocating, or physical ailments. I just trudged through, expecting that, at some point, I would no longer notice or care that I was sad, depressed, and lonely. I kept telling myself someday soon—I'll have time to grieve the death of my mother. Soon, I'll take the time to write those letters to friends going through hard times. I never did. I just kept moving about my life numb, zombified to my emotions.

So began the descent on my spiral staircase to take a peek inside. Three years of therapy and I still had high levels of anxiety. We went through m life history, talked all about my deceased mother, not having a father around my entire life, various relationships, my children, my spouse, etc. could talk all day about my circumstances—the truth is, that was another one of my strategies. If I spoke about it, and I didn't cry, get angry, or change the tone, that meant I was ok. I had many ways that I convinced myself I was ok. Nothing about me was ok. But my ego and brain weren't ready to concede. I could stay atop of my feelings, and still not feel them.

After having a panic attack in my therapy session and her asking me to wait in the lobby until I felt well enough to drive (because she didn't want to run over on our time!) I changed therapists. I finally felt something and took action. My therapist's choice will never make sense to me. I did feel abandoned by the one person I was paying to hang with me!

My new therapist Dale had an entirely different approach to our sessions. He offered tools for me to begin to feel. One was breath work; we would sit for half of our sessions breathing. He taught me how to breathe into my belly to help calm my parasympathetic system. He also had a way of listening to me which would tap directly into my emotions. He was my first teacher on emotional intelligence. I lived almost forty years without knowing what I was feeling. I had one default: SUPER ANGRY, otherwise known as rage. I would bottleneck everything inside and then explode.

You can see that this strategy was destined for disaster! Little by little I began to take moments of pause. I would start to feel something bubbling up inside of me, and instead of dismissing it, I became more curious; *why was I feeling this way? What was this feeling trying to show me?* It has taken years of practice and patience, splashed with humor. The interesting thing is that young children know themselves so well. They have an emotion; they allow it without regard to how it will look, or who it will offend. I learned to stuff my feelings into numerous bags, boxes, and purses. Only to allow my ugly out for the lucky ones, the people I was closest to. I'm sure they would see it another way, and this is why humor is important. Hiding is what brought me face to face with The Big Quiet.

There were people that I encountered in my life (Faith, her boyfriends, school children) who used their inadequacies as a way to make me feel less than, or unacceptable. Telling me I was "too emotional, too dramatic, too dumb, too fat, too sassy, too stupid, and too selfish." The truth that I now know is that every ounce of oneself is ok. It's learning how to polish the rough edges that takes practice.

Listening to my inner voice, learning to be with my judgments and harshness, until I grew a gentler way to speak to myself internally. Just as important as breathing through my belly, was learning how to talk to myself. To become my own friend and ally. Every new tool, experience, or teaching led me deeper inside. Reorganizing my internal home, decluttering the rooms, so that I could live in harmony with myself.

This was my opportunity to learn a more authentic way of being, no longer allowing the chaotic ways of the outer world to be ingested as my truth. I am working daily to rewire my emotional landscape so that it's no longer a landmine. Putting in LED lights, removing the harsh fluorescents, dialing down the radio channel from hard rock to slow jazz. I've become my best friend in this process. Seeing myself through a broader lens, allowing the nuances.

What began as terror and doom, gave me the chance to be rebirthed. Not as a hero of my story, as the observer. To see with more accuracy than I had in my troubled state, and to stop blaming others, or wait for someone to rescue me. No one could save me from me. Not one person. The big quiet wasn't here to help me be loved by others; it was here to help me love myself, despite how messy I was. To understand that to love the mess creates room to love the rest. Building a relationship with me was not easy, most days I wanted to give up, go back to pretending. And, there was this little curious voice inside me that wondered what it would be like if we only tried a little bit, and then a little bit more, and more... Until I could finally re-enter the world without fearing how I looked to anyone else but me.

If one would ask what was my best take away from the last four years, my reply; Presence. The presence of mind. Heart. Soul.

Making mud pies with Christina in the damp air of summer, playing hopscotch on the playground, learning how to ride a bike, or my first time roller skating. Feeling cool because my bike had a banana seat, they most likely were already out of style, but it was my first and only, so that made it especially cool! Jumping fences in our neighborhood and being chased by the homeowners, these were the moments I felt like a usual kid. I didn't have "stuff," I was just like everyone else. It was important to me to be like everyone else. Until one day, it no longer was....

Through my experience of The Big Quiet, I came into contact with several masks I was wearing to prove myself, keep myself safe and hidden. Once I saw them for what they were, they were no longer able to fit as snuggly as they once had in my psyche. My masks began to fall away and it was like losing a dear friend, someone who always brought you comfort, assurances, dependability. Dropping my masks was an introduction with my integrity. It became more of a compromise to wear the mask or carry it around with me, than to put it on for necessities sake. This choice unraveled the messy process of being me. Mind you, there are many selves to my personality depending on the day, my mood, the environment that I'm in, how well I've taken care of myself, etc. There are many different versions of me that can crop up. Some aspects of my shadow side are martyr, victim, unlovable, Zen/guru, despicable, anxious, lazy, and so many other fun-to-explore qualities.

While shedding of my masks I gave myself the time and opportunity to understand the rich architecture of my inner world, instead of bypassing who I am, what I need, and what I am projecting. At my core I am divine light. The way to it has been bumpy, wild, and downright oppressive at times. Maybe there's a smoother way to awaken, maybe I chose the hard way. It matters not. It was my way, and I am far more proud of the discoveries than any masks I once carried.

As my artfully crafted creations began dropping, I became more interested in hobbies and trying new things. I tried fencing, knitting, painting, hand drumming, volunteering, writing, and, little by little, I devoted my time to areas of interests that filled me up. They took time away from my normal day to day life, these hobbies that were the elixir my soul was craving. I slowly learned I didn't need to keep pulling energy from others to fill myself up; I turned the spigot off and found a main line to fulfillment. The masks were in the way of my experiencing life on my terms, at my pace, for my own enjoyment. I didn't need another person to tell me it was ok to do these things. I gave myself permission for the first time to explore who I really was.

Adam gave me the space to explore and be—though he wasn't always happy about my time away or, in a sense, being cut off from my experiences. Sharing verbally is not the same as first-hand experience. My explorations created more distance in our relationship, which, if I were looking to see this, would have been evidence of his love for me. He let me fly as far away as I needed to be with myself.

Of course, this is a high level of thinking that I didn't have at the time. I saw him as distant, shutting me out, disinterested in what I was creating. This is a pure projection of my own inner world. I was pushing off from the shore of our co-dependent coupling, to blaze a new trail in my life. I could have invited him, but I didn't. I wanted to search the wilderness on my own. I was seeking relics left behind by my future self that would help me in developing a sense of self-reliance. I didn't feel safe doing this in the face of another; I wanted to have only my perceptions of the experiences, without old opinions of who I was, or who I was known to be, coloring my new experiences. This choice may have seemed selfish, hurtful, and callous. Perhaps it was, and I did not believe there was another way. Early in my shedding and expanding I did invite friends, Adam, and even our children to join me. I would receive feedback that my interests were strange and uncomfortable for the other people accompanying me. I was moving at a fast pace in my growth spurt and it wasn't for someone else to keep up with, it was my path, and the speed in which I laid it was only for me. I was pioneering a new way of experiencing my life, without the constructs of safety being my main objective. I was seeking fulfillment, bliss.

During my nine-month re-birthing with HeatherAsh Amara of Warrior Goddess training, one of the favorite teachings I learned was a technique called stalking ourselves. It's a means to follow your patterns or habits in order to gain clarity of what is no longer working well or serving you.

I've been tracking and stalking my Joy. Joy is an elusive mythical creature that lives far away from the badlands of my heart. A long time ago I banished it from the tender places inside of me. It hurt too much to watch it appear and I couldn't appreciate or take delight in its company. I was in the hollows of my own suffering and joy wasn't a welcomed guest. Through growing a capacity for my own pain, furthermore, expanding into the healing of the pain, I came to realize that pain and joy are not adversaries, or incompatible. They can coexist quite well when allowed. It's a state of receptivity that creates the atmosphere for joy to be welcomed, even when life hurts.

As I have moved farther from the hollows, I am summoning more Joy into my life. I would also like for it to accompany play, laughter, ease, and grace. These qualities all have a similar spice, one that I reflexively contract in the face of. It's a worthiness issue, an old story that I've told myself for far too long. It started with me feeling that I didn't deserve happiness because I wasn't a good girl. This agreement came from a series of abusive traumas that I made to mean I deserve the abuse: *If I were better, I wouldn't have been violated.*

From this convoluted state, I had a gross misunderstanding of where joy lived. I smoked cigarettes that gave me a little taste of joy. Then I began drinking, one or two beers didn't bring joy, but a six-pack did. Then I turned to harder drugs, cocaine, ecstasy, acid—and I found joy. I hung around men that were rebellious and wild, thinking that, too, was a conduit of joy. After a stint of being isolated and alone, I came out of my drunken haze, realizing that the choices I was making drove me farther away from any true happiness I could encircle myself with. I learned that excess isn't where joy lives. It can't be found in substances.

Ah, let me try material things! I began shopping and antiquing. *Ah yes, I am back with joy, this is so fun!* Until my bookshelves, closets, cupboards, and house began to overflow with objects. Suddenly joy was once again elusive. Now I am decluttering and donating pounds, literal pounds, of items each month, to lessen the weight of material joy, which isn't feeling very joyful! It's cumbersome and embarrassing. Countless hours of my life spent perusing aisles of manufactured things.

The farther I walk with the intention of living from my joy, the more I see it fluttering about, like a hummingbird darting by. I catch a glimmer of it from the side of my eye. My body senses the presence of joy, and my thoughts soften. I stay in the moment, no matter how fleeting, to let joy know I am here and willingly receptive to a visit. I do not blame joy for being skittish. I did, after all, cast her away. It was my immaturity and lack of sight that negated this delightful relationship. One that I will spend the rest of my breaths trying to cultivate once more, extending my hand to the silent dancer, if only to be graced on my fingertips.

My desire is to continue my healing journey and sharing from a place of exploration, inviting others to join me, in circle, virtually or in person; fostering places of solace in a time when we feel disjointed and alone. I have this deep sense of trust that all is working for our favor. It is hard to share this publicly because it isn't the consensus. To come to this state of trust, also, comes a state of acceptance. I accept that I can't control the circumstances in our world. I can only control being a conscious contributor in our world. One way I do this is by devoting me to maintaining the highest frequency possible, while continuing to grow my capacity for higher vibrations. My reason for this is to entrain others to this frequency which can help to heal our planet. I believe in this deeply, knowing that it is the most I can give. It's what I want for our family, friends and the world. To know they are safe, healed, whole and accepted in any state they arrive. We are all here to experience life. One of the greatest successes isn't our wealth; it's our investment in brightening the world. Letting our lights shine forth, and keeping our hearts open for connection. This how I determine success.

When people ask, "Who are you?" I want to say; "I am Brigid the Illuminator. I am an artist of the soul, and my life is an expression of my art."

"Shhhh, walk quieter!"

"I am!"

"Shhhh, don't yell."

"I'm not!"

"Brigid, seriously we don't want to get caught, try to be quiet."

"I ammmmm being quiet, you're the one who keeps talking to me!"

Kate and I, and a few others, made our way down the deer trail. We settled in our usual spot. Tonight was going to be epic! We had more processed cheese than ever before. This was a favorite pastime of ours. We would sit along the Shore way late at night and wait for cars to come under the overpass.

The Shore way runs parallel to Lake Erie. There were seldom police patrolling the area; though occasionally Rangers would pass by. I was working at a concession stand at the beach and knew most of them. I had a false sense of security about our illegal activities. It seemed perfectly innocent to us to fling processed cheese squares at cars. It was always a mission to see who would get the most direct hits, as most of our cheese ended up on the Shore way. It was our way of being rebellious without doing damage, a dance of youthful folly. Most cars went by in the night, never seeing the impending cheese; others would hit their brakes momentarily and keep going.

It was the moment in between the cheese leaving my fingers and waiting, in stop-motion, to see if it would hit the car. I could count the time as the cheese hung in the air. The whole group would hush once the cheese was flung. Then we would exhale and break out in mad laughter!

The ruts that are worn
Come from a sense of comfort
Repetition
Endurance to live is not living
The harder the waves crash upon your shores
The stronger the calling to soften
Open
Listen
Invite in possibility
Things are ever changing
Impermanent
The illusion of grabbing
Digging
Or rutting in
Will not change the intensity
It will not protect one from
Inevitability
What is meant for you
Will come
Either as a gentle breeze
Or high tide
There is choice
There is control
It's not outside of you
Though
It's in your heart
Honoring
What is true for you
Not what you "should do"
Who you "should be"
What looks good to him, her, or me
Heave yourself out of the rut
Get comfortable with
Being uncomfortable

Let life see that you are no longer adversaries
But a team
One can never know how grand the view
When buried up to their neck in distorted sight
Give life your hand
Let it lead you
The end is the same for all of us
Choosing possibility
Pleasure
Mystery
That is a portal for those living above the rut

Happiness is a large concept for me; it's not a place I thought I would actively seek out. I told myself that it belonged to them, *those people.* Anyone but me, I truly believed I was dealt a life that would be painful until my last breath. I wanted more, but I didn't believe I deserved it. Even Adam, has a joke (that I no longer find humorous); that he "found me in the gutters and saved me." I mean what the hell kind of joke is that to tell?! I didn't believe I needed saving at the time. I thought he was grand, and we would have a good life. I didn't realize that I was on the quick slope my mother had shown me of being more interested in a high than connection. I enjoyed partying most nights, working a dead-end job, and creating drama any time that I could. I did this to keep reminding myself that I mattered; drama was the card in my pocket that I pulled when I had the pesky feelings rise within. I believed the drama showed me how important I am. If people would engage in a fight, gossip, cry, be outraged with me or at me, it meant that I was seen, I had value. I worked hard to stow away pesky feelings as far down as they would settle. I didn't want to feel them, I was tired of feeling how hard life was.

Faith would excitedly tell me this story, I heard it many times growing up. Maybe it was her way of curing me into my intuition: When I was born and she would leave me in the cradle, whenever she came back into the room the cradle would be rocking and she could smell my Great Grandmother's gardenia scented perfume throughout the air.

I believe I've always been connected to spirit. I used to be able to see spirits. As I aged that freaked me out, but I could still feel their presence and sometimes hear them. I could always tell someone how many ghosts lived in their house...wasn't the most welcomed conversation!

Our friends Nichol and Jason lived in a house in Lakewood. Whenever Adam and I would spend the night there I would have tormented dreams. Often, I would wake soaked in sweat and frightened. I remember one time Nichol came in from an event and she went up to bed. I stopped in to say goodnight and the room must have been 15 degrees colder than the rest of the house. I could see my breath when I spoke to hear. She told me it was normal and that the room was always this cold! I had an eerie feeling in that room and in the basement. There would be times that cabinet doors would open and close in their kitchen. After several unexplainable events they decided to look into the history of their house. They came to find out that a young man, maybe under the age of 20, hung himself in the basement.

Looking back throughout my life I can see what a blessing it was to have "real" imaginary friends. They were the people I could talk to through all of the uncertainty. There was a little hand that I would often feel on my right shoulder, a steady presence that everything would be ok, no matter what was taking place at that moment. I felt assured that the presence was here to help me and wouldn't lead me astray!

During a personal development circle my teacher; Debi shared a story about a Chinese airline being sued by the F.A.A. because they didn't tell the passengers to put on their own oxygen masks before assisting other passengers in the event of an emergency. It never occurred to them because it was something they inherently knew. I was in awe of this story. She was sharing it in the context of: If you want to be a medium, you first need to help yourself! What seems so basic was a foreign concept to me! "You mean it is ok to consider my own needs first?" I had heard the message countless times during my own travels, but this was the first time it meant something to me.

Living a survival lifestyle came with certain layers of excitement. I believe it was my convoluted idea of what fun is. Or what thrills can be thought of as fun, that I am still trying to create drama in my life. I find that when things are good, calm, and connected, I push off and create a storm. The storm is where I find comfort. I know this place well. I know my strengths here. Except that when the storm passes, I fall into deep shame and guilt over how I've acted. Then I hold onto the shame and guilt because they too are familiar. These cycles have been present in my life for as long as I can recall. It sickens me to finally put all of the pieces together and see it as a whole system—a system of codependency that I keep in motion, to protect myself. The pressure of not creating drama is greater than initiating the dramas. The quiet and grandeur of a happy life scares me more than everything I've noted above. If I give myself over to them, what do I have to assure myself of my strengths? What do I have to remind myself that it's safe here? The storms I create on some strange level bring me comfort, a sense of safety. Happiness leaves me exposed, suspended in time. Wondering, *when it leaves, can I survive?*

Feeling passions and desires is a place I am growing capacity. Like a pair of pants that once were too big, now more comfortable and form fitting. I've always had an affinity for beautiful things. One of the many reasons I love the Cleveland Museum of Art is that it's loaded with beauty. I can walk the halls for hours staring at the brush strokes of famous works. The dedication one has for their craft makes me weep.

Through all of the experiences we had in our lives, I had a constant friend. One that helped me to keep waking up for another day, eager to see what it held for me. Hope, another feeling state was a best friend to me. I would share secrets with her, tell her my dreams, and she would soothe my worries. Reminding me that when the sun rises, the slate is restored to new. I needn't worry about yesterday. Hope encouraged me to write, use a camera, draw, become a parent, and become a wife.

My biggest dream as a little girl was to be an actress or a nurse. I wanted to help people and I loved drama. Aunt Mary used to take me to see The Glenn Miller Band, and on our drive to and from the theatre, she would tell me about other performers she liked or movies she was fond of. I would keep an eye out and watch everything I could when they showed it on T.V. I became a fan of Fred Astaire and Ginger Rogers movies. Faith always loved Mae West. I didn't like her sensuality at the time. It made me uncomfortable. Ginger, however, was a class act. My favorite was/is Audrey Hepburn. She was a work of art; in her demeanor, humanitarianism, and grace. It was her grace that most caught my affections. My hope is to present grace such as she did in the world. Perfuming the world of grace is a legacy, and worthy of my aspirations.

Can we talk about PTA groups, please?! When the kids were young and we were still acclimating to living back in Cleveland, I began seeking connection, and thought it would be a good idea to join early childhood PTA groups, or some type of community organization that would help me meet women with children around the age of mine. I had high expectations that this could be one place of shared interests to begin a friendship. Don't get me wrong; all of the people I have met from these groups are wonderful people. I did, however, find one commonality no matter what group I belonged to: a pressure to be something I am not. To pretend to be a model parent, perfect family, or know what the hell I am doing. I don't know what I am doing! I am trying to enjoy days that are unmanageable and be at peace when there is little to be found.

It was Halloween and we were attending a party as a family. It was hosted through the early childhood PTA group. I was super excited because Adam didn't usually enjoy forced interaction events. We were all set; Adam dressed as a vampire, me as a witch, and the kids in their character costumes, a princess and a knight. Off we went. When we got to the hall, we quickly realized that we were not in character. All of the parents were dressed in sweet, non-scary costumes. Adam had blood dripping from his mouth; I had dramatic witch makeup on. It felt like the music stopped and everyone was glaring at us, and bringing their children closer to them, in horror of what had just arrived.

We are the type of parents and people who are old-school and thought adding details to the costumes would make the more believable, not realizing that it may have been inappropriate. Still trying to navigate this new world of group activities with young children, we were proud to arrive as a family in full costume, as it took a lot for everyone to get ready and be in the spirit of the holiday. After that night, it became apparent to me to read all materials thoroughly!

One might say the problem with me is I say what needs to be said, whether you want to hear it or not. I've been called a destabilizer. I prefer to think of it as not beating around the bush, also, being trustworthy. Maybe being a straight shooter is a defect, a curse, or the greatest gift for one to receive. Society asks that we follow along and play nice, fair and blend. I can't blend; I'm neon in a box of pastels. I stopped volunteering at the school events and pretending to have nice conversations about chocolate chip cookies and the next book fair. Hello, my marriage is falling apart and my kid hates me! I really don't care about the latest recipe. I needed to be seen where I was, and not worry about the okayness of it. I am a real person, facing real life circumstances and being able to talk with other women about this is important to me. The reason we were gathering didn't assure connection. We were there for the kids, not us. I think that is a failing of a community gathering. We should be able to have earnest conversations and feel supported. Of course the children matter, and what matters more is that the parents are balanced, supported and connected. That there are more than four sets of eyes on an entire family. Maybe I am disillusioned by the old saying; "It takes a village." I really believe it does take a village, and when you see one of them laying on the sidelines worn thin by the demands of life, step in and step up to assist. Listen to the story, give a hug, anything.

I never expect someone to fix my situation. Being seen and listened to help me turn a corner and see the same problem with new insights because I had the chance to speak it, and not carry it around in my head. I'd like to believe it helps other women and men, too. To know that some days just suck! Sometimes marriage is daunting, and it's hard to know if you'll ever get out of a rut. Talking to seasoned vets in marriage helps. Everyone has something to offer another, if only we take the time to drop the mask and be with them.

I met Jillian the first year Alex began kindergarten. We both sat in the orientation and had polite conversation, and though it took several years of me persistently inviting her to be friends, she inevitably caved! I think what may have sealed the deal was our mutual fascination of being on a planet floating through space. Why people take time to plant grass is beyond my comprehension!

We were headed to Southern Tier Brewery in western New York. We had the whole weekend to ourselves for a girl's get-away. It was the second time I had been away from my family for more than a few hours. I was super excited to visit the brewery and go to the spa. As we were wrapping up our day at the spa, one of the pedicurists suggested we go to the Audubon Society for their Reiki day. "What is Reiki?" I asked. She said something about energy work that it's relaxing and we would love it. It sounded good to us! We looked on the map and saw it wasn't far from us. We stopped off for lunch and then made our way there. When we entered, you could feel the Zen-ness float by on the slight breeze we brought in. There were diffusers going and low lighting, everyone was whispering and chill music was playing in the background. We signed in and excitedly took our seats.

I met my practitioner and she explained the process: Lay down on the table, she may use light touch on my body, and I may see colors or feel warmth as she gives me Reiki. I agreed, and she began. As I lay on the table I drifted to another place entirely. I was new to Reiki, and I may have only meditated a few times prior to that day. I was still on the external, and not too terribly interested in sitting still for too long. In my dreamy state I saw waves of colors, and images of things I didn't know. I would somewhat come back to the room, and drift again. After she was done, she spoke to me of the trauma that occurred to my pelvis and that my heart hung heavy from a relationship issue. She said she sent a lot of healing energy to my pelvis and it should begin feeling better. Also, to have a phone call with the person who is affecting my heart.

Jillian and I floated out of the center. We were giggling and Zen tipsy over how far out that experience was. We sat in her car for a bit to get back to ourselves before driving. We both had unique experiences that were personal to each of us. It was the best $20 Reiki session of my life!

That experience hung with me for several months. I noticed things were slightly different upon my return. I had a sincere interest in creating more harmony in my life. I picked up a book by Deborah King, *The Truth Heals*. She is a world-renowned Master Energy Healer and teacher. Her book was stirring and complex for me, as I knew nothing about Chakras, or how we store traumas in our body. I was opening to a curiosity that wouldn't be fully ripe for another few years. It took me time to begin listening to the call from within. Though we didn't know where that experience would lead us, it was my initiation into the world of holistic healing.

A difficulty in my journey is making the decision to honor what is best for me. It feels similar to turning a yacht around with a toothpick, having no use of a Rutter or map by which to orient. I used to gain much pleasure from pleasing other people. Pleasing others gave me a sense of being necessary and valuable. I've let go of that behavior, to become a different version of myself no matter what. I let go of opportunities, relationships, popularity, expectations of how I show up, who I show up for and in what state I arrive! All in the name of orienting my compass to the direction of my heart. Not one single thing I left, or had to walk away from, was easy or without some form of pain. Most of the time when a person begins to grow it leaves the people around them slightly more vulnerable, equally so for me, it is a difficult balance of growing, and being seen where you are now and not who you were. I found it too difficult to balance at times, and most likely made matters worse between myself and another. It wasn't intentional as much as necessity. Growing into a new person takes energy and consistency. It takes time for everything to naturally work itself out. Where once I used force, I now know time and grace are a natural remedy.

Every hard conversation, face of disappointment, or silence that fell, in what was once a dynamic relationship, inevitably led me to discernment. From this place of discernment, I am honoring my path, my magic, and the potency by which I deliver my gifts. Being purposeful and conscientious of how I use my time is what allows me room to deepen my craft and service to others. I am devoted to my spiritual life, the lessons that come along the way. It may not be for everyone. It is my chosen path.

The interesting part of bravery is no one will truly know just how hard it was for you, but you. And, that isn't what makes you brave.

You knew how hard it was, and still moved forward.

Chapter Five
Jerry Springer Would Blush

What I am about to reveal has all been told through other people's perspectives. I wasn't alive when this part of my story began. It's a part of our family's skeletons that helps to explain how far people will go to save face. I have been the recipient of the choices, as were others. I am sharing this to expose the power that shame has when we continue to feed into it.

Faith was raised during an era when women were expected to play certain roles; to keep the home tidy, tend to the children, and keep their husband satisfied. The flames that burned inside of her were evident in her desires. She had aspirations and was shunned, shamed, and dismissed. As a mother, I know that I have done the same thing to my own daughter. There were times that her passions burned so hot that all of my own insecurities were presented between us. I couldn't support her passions because I wasn't supporting my own. I wasn't a big enough person to put all of her before me. I can only assume that something along those lines was present between Faith and Bobo. They had a history that the whole family referred to as dysfunctional. What I know is that Faith mourned the passing of her mother every day until they were reunited the day she passed, May 15, 2006. I choose to believe that she saw her mother again after her last breath was shared with me.

Faith liked to party even as a young lady; she and my Aunt Mary would go to the Irish American club and dance their hearts out. The two of them loved to have fun and be lighthearted. At some point, Faith intermingled with a married man named Ed. The way I understand it, he was a family acquaintance that Faith took a shine to, and vice versa. She ended up having an affair with Ed, and became pregnant with twins; although they didn't know they were twins at the time. Bobo, my grandmother, was furious at this situation and absolutely would not allow the family to be shamed by Faith's immorality. Aunt Mary said she forced Faith to have an abortion. Back in the early 1950's abortions weren't performed in the hospital. You had to know a guy, who knows a guy. Faith was sent away to "visit family." While away, she had a botched abortion that only terminated one of the fetuses. To her and Bobo's surprise, she ended up having a boy. Faith was terribly ill, as she had an infection from the procedure, which put her and the baby in jeopardy. They didn't know it at the time that she was still carrying. The sweet innocent boy came into world on March 23 and was raised mostly by our Great Grandmother May, and occasionally by Faith. I am unclear if this was by choice, irresponsibility or both. Here is where it gets tricky and the skeletons begin to accrue in the closet...

As I was growing up, Uncle Gerry was often present. He had bouncy black curls and dimples that complimented his bright smile in such a way that I always wanted to have dimples. He was attentive, mostly kind with me. It was in my later years I thought of him as my guardian angel. We were close to him on and off in my early years, sharing different residences. One day I knew that he would no longer be near us. I never knew the details. Faith told me that our Uncle Gerry wouldn't be visiting us anymore, that he hated me, and her.

The day of my mother's wake I was standing alongside the casket, and a woman arrived with a younger woman. Both looked familiar, but I couldn't quite place who they were. The older woman approached first, with a gentle smile and look that showed me how happy she was to see me.

"Hello, Brigid we are so sorry to hear of Faith's passing."

"Thank you, how did you know Faith?" She now looked at the younger woman with the shiny black hair dark as an espresso bean.

"You don't remember us?" she asked.

"I'm sorry, I don't."

"I'm your Aunt Mary and this is your cousin Sharon."

"Oh!" I was quite surprised as I did recall who they are, but I couldn't place their faces. Time had passed for each of us and I hadn't seen them since I was no more than 10 years old.

Sharon, my cousin, was always a glowing teenager that I wished I looked like. She had long black silky hair and deep brown almond shaped eyes. I loved listening to her stories about watching John Lennon's cat in London and meeting famous musicians. She had an air of fame and mystery to me. My Aunt Mary would pick me up once in a while and take me to see The Glenn Miller Band movies at the Lakewood Theater. I loved the smells and feel of that old theater. It seemed much older to me because of its sticky decor; a well-worn forest green rug and striped wallpaper. I can remember the sound of popcorn kernels exploding in the background and fountain pops being poured always had a hissing sound. I cherished our time together, as I never knew exactly where we were going. It was exciting to have someone surprise me. She would often take me for Chinese food either before or after the movie. I was needy for attention and she noticed.

As we continued catching up, we moved away from the casket and spoke about more recent happenings in our lives. I shared that I was about two months pregnant and already a mother of two. I introduced them to Adam. The children were with Adam's parents; their involvement helped tremendously, as losing Faith—what I thought was left of my family—was more difficult than I had anticipated, especially since we barely spoke the two years leading up to this. Welcoming her back into my life was a mourning of a different kind. Then I was mourning any hope of a connected and normal mother-daughter relationship. The roles we adopted early in our relationship were well worn and pointless to change when she was already ailing. At Adam's insistence, I invited Faith back into our lives Christmas of 2010. We shared Christmas, St. Patrick's Day, Easter, and a morphine drip on Mother's Day. I am thankful for all of it. Adam was right; I would have regretted not making contact with her before her passing. The last 30 minutes with my Mother gave me the opening to forgiveness and compassion, something I couldn't access during her life.

While Aunt Mary is still talking, I'm lost in these thoughts, and finally come back to the room.

"Where is your brother?" She asked with a tone of insistence. "And, why did you have the wake here? We always bury our family through McGorray Funeral Home."

The last time I heard that name was Bobo's funeral. I push those memories to the back of my mind. I remember Uncle Tony and Faith were very angry with Uncle Gerry showing up too late to her funeral.

The priest now ushers us to our seats as he is ready to offer a prayer. I look at her with a puzzled look. I had no idea why she was asking me about a brother. I'm an only child, I was certain she knew that.

As the priest is speaking she leans to my right ear and asks again, "Where is your brother, Gerry?"

I turn to her and say, "What are you talking about? Gerry is my *Uncle*, not my brother. I haven't spoken to him in years, almost as long as you and I have been estranged."

"Brigid, Gerry is your brother—why are you saying he is your Uncle?"

Now we are both confused, and completely missing the words the priest is sharing about Faith and her involvement with his Parish. I have no memory of what the priest said or the prayer spoken. I was swimming in the confusion Aunt Mary had just delivered.

"I grew up knowing a man named Uncle Gerry with curly brown hair and big cheeks, is this the Gerry you are speaking of?"

"Yes that he is your brother Gerry, why are you calling him your Uncle?"

"I only know him as my Uncle," I said.

"Is your Dad here?"

I know I shot her a look that said: *Ok time to pack it up, lady!*

"I never knew my father; do you know who he is?"

"Brigid this is all terribly confusing! He lives nearby, I am sure he would come to say goodbye if he knew, just like Gerry."

While I was reeling in my confusion, now I felt in some way to have disappointed her.

"I have no way of contacting Gerry. The last I heard, he hated us and never wanted to see us again. It never occurred to me that he would want to be here. As for my Dad, I was told he died in a car crash, only to later be told that was a lie. I haven't a clue who my Father is, or how to reach him."

She apologized profusely for bringing all of this up today, as she hadn't known the lies I was told, the secrets kept, or why.

During the break, I shared tiny bits with Adam and Nichol. I was feeling quite stirred and upset. I needed to care for myself, as being in the first trimester of pregnancy was difficult, and coupled with these stressors, I needed a break. Adam looked after Alex and Mae while Nichol and I went for a bite to eat. As we were talking she was extremely happy for me. To have all of this come to light was encouraging, as I was afraid of being the last successor of my family. I wasn't feeling as excited. I was deeply hurt that Faith chose to hide these things from me. It was my right to know my Dad with or without her involvement, the same with my brother. Why was he known to me as my Uncle? This was a time for a stiff drink and a nap. Neither was convenient currently.

We visited with more friends and family for the second viewing. Faith was active with her Parish in her later years. There were several people that I'd never met but spoke highly of her. I always admired her charisma and charm. She may never have known in her own heart, but to the many who loved her, she was lovable.

The priest offered closing words and final prayers for the viewing. As I held Adam's hand tightly, the priest walked over and closed the casket. In an instant, a lifetime was sealed beneath the silk. Is there thread fine enough to nestle one's lifetime?

My heart cracked; all the years of pretending nothing hurt, that I didn't care, acting like I would be fine with or without her --it was all a lie to protect me from this moment. It didn't work! My heart was cracking and there was nothing I could do but let it. It was just like Grandma Bobo's death. *How would I know that I am safe? That I will be ok? How am I to mourn the last part of my lineage?* It had been the two of us for so long. At that moment I could understand how Faith felt at losing her mother. All of the issues faded away, only love was present. I loved her and still do, the only way I know how, which is full spectrum? I hated, disliked, and detested the things she did to us. I loved, admired, and appreciated everything she tried to instill in me. I recalled the countless drunken episodes where she would sing me ridiculous songs and tell me fables that didn't make any sense. It was the gleam in her eyes that I will miss most. When she was happy or enthused about anything, something as simple as a sunny day, her eyes would sparkle. That is what I will always remember. She was human. She was struggling and she still found a reason to sparkle.

The lid latched; my heart cracked open and tears rimmed my eyelids when I was certain no more could be spared. Adam, Nichol, Aunt Mary, and Cousin Sharon all encircled me and Faith. There aren't words that soothe the soul in a time of loss; what helps is pure presence. Being with someone when they have nothing to offer, nothing to say, and extending your hands. That helps.

After my emotions settled, Aunt Mary brought in a large oil painting. I wasn't sure why she brought a painting to the wake? It looked like a picture of Shirley Temple; sweet ringlets strung together with a blue bow. Red cheeks and dimples, eyes that shimmered and glowing skin, it was a beautiful painting.

"I found this at an antique shop, as Sharon and I love to go antiquing. When I saw it I knew exactly who it was and had to have it. When I told the antique dealer that it used to hang in my Great Aunt's home, that the girl is my cousin, she gave me a good price for it."

"Wait—is that painting of Faith when she was a little girl?"

"Yes, this was a commissioned piece, done for Aunt May, which hung in their parlor for many years. When she died, a lot of the estate was sold off, and this painting made its way to an antique shop not far from here."

I was completely blown away! I have very few things from of our families. I had two pictures of myself as a child. *My entire childhood, two pictures!* We moved so often and had little resources growing up that takin photos was a luxury. It wasn't something I even noticed or thought of in my youth. This painting was a treasure!

Weeks after the service, I reached out to friends of mine that still had connections in the debt collections industry, and they were able to help me locate his last known address. They had found three different addresses for him. I cast a wide net, mailing the letters to my assumed brother. In the letter I shared of my current life situations, living in Cleveland, married, two, soon to be three, children. That I wasn't looking for anything other than to acknowledge his rightful title and place in my life, I wanted to assure him that my character wasn't tarnished by being raised to adulthood by Faith. Not knowing the reasons of his departure from our lives, it was important that he know I meant no harm or would impose in anyway in his current life.

Within a week of mailing the letter, I received a phone call from his wife, Linda. She was surprised to hear from me. The thing I recall the most was her saying; "Gerry is so relieved to know you are ok. He worried about you for years. Your brother loves you very much!" She spoke of things that I vaguely recalled. I wanted to remember all of the times we spent together. To feel a sense of connection and closeness, I was still in my own honeycomb of mourning; sticky, messy, and stingingly sweet.

Faith had a habit of being vain. She hid her age as well as her secrets. No one ever knew how old she really was. Gerry, my brother-uncle, was a secret from me. Not my family. I will never know why she didn't tell me he was her son. I can only assume it would disclose her approximate age, which was a well-guarded secret. I have another theory. She was ashamed of how I came to be. If I knew he was my brother than I would certainly know how old my father was at the time of their affair. Through Aunt Mary's research and later confirmation from Gerry, I found out the details of my origin. I was conceived through a relationship that was taboo and possibly illegal. Faith fell in love with Gerry's best friend. He was still in high school at the time. This relationship destroyed any hope of my brother respecting or trusting Faith again. His best friend was my father, John Heyer Jr. They were high school seniors. To be generous, he most likely was 18 years old, still young, and difficult to know if he was ready to commit to being a husband and father. That part of my story will stay buried with the two of them. John died just a few years before Faith, in October of 2001, a few days after his 54th birthday.

The man I spoke of earlier, Chad, who came to celebrate my 13th birthday, was a part of this plot twist, as Faith was hanging out and intimate with him during her romance with my father. Chad was also a friend of my brother's. Either Chad assumed, or was told, that he was my father. Though I never had blood tests taken to confirm or deny who my true father is, it can all be attested for in my facial features and eyes.
 Oddly, my birth certificate has another elusive party's name; "Max Joseph". I am not sure of his affiliation to our family, or Faith. I am fairly certain that he wasn't my father. Gerry told me I look very similar to John. For several years after our reunion, he would take me out to a restaurant and we would celebrate our birthdays together, seeing as we were both born in March, surprisingly only 3 days apart.

During one of our dinners I asked him, "Does it hurt you to see me? Do I remind you of things you wished to no longer remember?"

He said, "You do look just like John, the best parts; his eyes and his kindness. Those things feel good to remember."

It was a difficult question to ask, but also, it relieved my heart. I will never know all that he endured being with Faith during his upbringing. It's for him to share, not for me to impose upon. My wish is to not be a reminder of times that he would rather forget. Thankfully we have both put those bones to rest.

I remember my Dad, as it was his hand I held that day at Kiddie Park. He was the man with the flannel shirt and safe smile. He was the only friend of Faith's I felt safe with growing up. I don't recall exactly how old I was when he stopped visiting. I have two pictures of him; the one in my heart, and the one in my memory. We visit him every year for Father's Day and Christmas.

The misgiving about shame is trying to hide from it does more damage than exposing it. I missed the chance to grow up with a brother. I missed the chance to fill in the hole in my heart and psyche left from not having my Dad. I believed that I wasn't lovable or worthy to be loved because my Dad didn't stay. This only came to my knowledge after the incident with Chad on my 13th birthday. In some strange way, I may never have felt abandoned or unfulfilled in my heart, if I still believed that my father died in a car crash. But, once I found out that Faith had lied and that Chad wasn't my dad, and my dad didn't die, it left me with a pile of misgivings to sort through the rest of my life. I know now it wasn't simple, nor did his choice have anything to do with me. He was taking care of himself, just as Faith was trying to protect or care for some part of her. The truth heals even when it's hard. Shame is a liar.

It was the summer of 1984, Kelli was visiting, and Faith had big plans for us that day. We were going to see her doctor. Now one might ask, why is this a big day? Oh, that's where this gets fun! This doctor was an unusual variety. He helped fat people get thin. It wasn't done through hypnosis or talk therapy—no he had a much quicker and more effective weight loss plan. Faith spent hours the night before packing pennies in little brown tubes. Every Time she finished she had a look of exaltation on her face. I noticed what she was doing but didn't realize their intended purpose. Kelli and I were playing in the courtyard when Faith called us in. She excitedly told us that we were going on an adventure today. We were going to the Eastside of town to see her doctor. Needless to say, we were not as excited as she was. I kept asking why we had to go with her; I was 13 at the time and felt more than responsible enough to stay home.

"Well who is going to wear all the pennies?" she asked.

"What do you mean 'wear all the pennies'?"

"I need you and Kelli to help me at the doctors. The pennies will help weigh you down, and he will think you AND Kelli need weight loss supplements."

My protests fell on deaf ears. I had no interest in being her mule, helper, or reason for getting more of *those* pills, and now she is trying to use my friend, too!

We spent the next hour being loaded down with rolls of pennies that were taped around our bellies, shoved in our bras and the front and back of our upper thighs. She wanted to be certain he wouldn't detect any funny business if we had to wear a gown. Every step was surreal. I felt that I was walking in another person's body. Nothing felt familiar to me. I was not burdened by pennies alone; the shame and embarrassment of having her for my mother weighed most heavily on my mind.

The building was large, with a big cafeteria on the main floor. We rode the elevator to his office. As we waddled down the hallway, one of the overhead lights flickered and buzzed. It gave an eerie feel to the place. His office was packed with people, most of whom weren't "fat" with pounds, but addiction. Everyone twitched and tapped little beads of sweat on the brow lines. It was a seedy place and we were Faith's accomplices to her addiction. Oblivious to what the addiction was at the time, but I knew enough that not one part of this scenario was normal or ok!

She told the doctor that we were her nieces visiting and we were both over 18. *Doesn't everyone take their relatives who are in town to get checked out for weight loss supplements?!* He never checked our I.D. or asked many questions. He took me back first. She accompanied me—most likely to be assured I didn't blow the whole operation! He asked me to take off my shoes and step on the scale, and then he measured my height. Based on two simple measurements, he was certain I needed to lose at least 20 pounds in order to be "healthy". Kelli was next and the same applied to her, although she needed to lose slightly less weight. As we walked out of the office, and down the dingy hall that kept more secrets than a journal, Faith was giddy—so pleased with herself that her plan was foolproof. What she hadn't thought about in her planning was the disgust I would be left to bear after she swallowed her happy pill. When we arrived back home, we began unpacking our weight. I still felt 30 pounds heavier, even after the last roll was removed. I would never see her as my hero again. She sickened me, and all I could see was her weakness.

The day she died, they handed me all of her belongings. Inside of her bag was a box of Sudafed. Faith could no longer supply her addiction to the more pure amphetamine, Black Beauty that the doctor was handing out like gumballs back in the 80's. She worked her way down to over the counter stimulants as the years clicked on. Somehow it seemed more respectable to have a constant need for stimulant-loaded decongestants than street drugs.

A revelation occurred sometime after Faith's death. I was reading an article in the paper about Imodium A-D being used by people with opioid addiction. When taking a high dose of this product, apparently you can get high. Faith was masterful at getting high. I never understood why she would take boxes of Imodium each day, boxes! Nor did it make sense for her to ask me to bring her the pills because she couldn't get them at the pharmacy for being over the limit. None of it ever raised a red flag, because why would someone overdose on anti-diarrhea medication?! My jaw dropped reading the article, as all of the weird fragmented pieces came together!

Faith was always concerned with her appearance, especially her weight. The drive to be thin was so intense for her that she not only ridiculed me and my appearance my entire life, but also was an early pioneer in bariatric surgery. I believe she had it shortly after I was born. I never remember her having surgery for that during my youth. The problems that she encountered were severe. She would occasionally remark to me that I should have the surgery. Outraged at her suggestion, I remember asking why she would suggest this absurdity to me after her experience, and if given the choice now, would she do it again, she said yes! That floored me. She became so ill that she almost died when I was a teenager. This time it wasn't at the hand of my step-father, James. She was no longer absorbing nutrients, as a great portion of her small intestines were removed during the procedure. They didn't know at the time that malabsorption would become a complication. I would sit in the waiting room while she would get magnesium injections that made her scream. They also gave her countless IV supplements of vitamins and other nutrients to help her overall health. The fact she made it to her 67th year of life was miraculous, although, I am still unsure if that is her correct age, as she never told the truth about that detail of her life.

Chapter Six

Bricks and Mortar

What does home mean to you? I have a distortion of home. I can think of it in the physical sense, using my address to symbolize home. Because we moved often in my life, being identified by one residence doesn't feel like home to me. We bought the home Adam's grandmother and grandfather built. This house was their home. They designed it, loved it, and spent many happy years here. The first time I walked through her door, I too loved this house. Every time after, I had the same feeling, until she passed away. We had two young children and one would be conceived soon thereafter. We were more than happy to buy this house and build a life here. We are going on our fifteenth year and this house doesn't feel like home.

What is Home?

Words
Eyes
Doors
The Sun
Inner connection
How far will I roam before I find it
Is it with me, always
Do I create it
Is it a fixed structure
or
Fluid thought
Can home be felt and never truly known
Is that true for love
Is love only known through feeling, not thought
Does it ever belong to anyone
Anything
Can it be contained
Or does it roam as freely as the wind
Or bob on the oceans rhythmic tide
These experiences we try to capture, contain, remember

Are imprinted in memory
Not to be stored
To be treasured
As in friendship
I may never know all of you
Understand what brings a smile to your face
Any gust of your essence
Is a graced moment to be placed
In memory

The closest I have come to home was standing in the Pacific Ocean. The salty waters of the Pacific felt like home, as did the enormous Redwoods. Both of those places held me energetically like nothing I've experienced since. A piece of my primal self knows that location is my ancestral home. Some of my heritage lived on Achill Island, Ireland. We were sea people. I know this all may sound a bit odd, but hear me out. If we walked through life, only identifying with things based on feeling, can you imagine how different your life might look? I was certain I wanted a home, fence, dogs, nice cars, etc.... None of it has felt good. Everything I have in my life is nice, given with generosity, and I receive it. And yet, there is a beckoning that lives within me that has been unanswered. It's the wilder, untamed part of me. Living as a gypsy with Faith was difficult; there was no pattern, no certainty, and little safety. Yet, it satisfied my wild self.

Home may be a symbol of responsibility. This is something I am still working on. What if the life we live is based on the premise of responsibility that only pleases a system, not the individual? Why do I have to do certain things in order to be warm, fed, and sheltered? If I were living on my own, it would be my responsibility to meet these based on my own timeline and necessity. This isn't the same layer as a societal responsibility.

Faith struggled to meet these responsibilities which I theorize drove some of her addiction issues. She felt an enormous amount of pressure that she couldn't meet. We lived in cars, homes of strangers—I am sure Faith knew the people, I didn't. Upgraded to hotel and motel rooms, finally resting in larger apartments—which we shared with roaches. Have you ever had to deal with roaches? I give those little fuckers credit. They are the most determined thing on the planet. They will survive despite poison, heat, suffocation, starvation, dehydration. There is very, and I mean very, little one can do to drive out a roach infestation. They take over everything. The most revolting part was opening a drawer or cabinet and finding the next generation had hatched, left behind were the remnants of their egg sacks. Little ovals that was papery and brown. They would fumigate the apartment about every six months, and we would watch them pour out from one apartment complex, and run into another. During those times, I would have elected for a car or stranger's house. One time I was being picked up for a date by a well-dressed, mannered, and wealthy young man named Chris. I adored him; he was a poet, and very romantic. I was now 15 and budding. He came to the apartment to meet Faith and James, and as they were asking Chris the details of our evening, Fat Freddy crawled up the wall. Freddy was the biggest of the roach gang that patrolled our apartment. I was mortified—I knew by now that not everyone had a roach gang they cohabitate with. Chris was a gentleman and most likely more aware of the circumstances I pretended to not notice. There was no way he could miss Freddy! While we had a "home" it wasn't comfortable. Our residence on W. 117th was a time in my life I almost felt "shanty Irish", the gift of my lineage was to be higher than our reality. We appeared better than we were, it wasn't ego, and it was inflation, a means to float when it would otherwise be natural to sink.

Where I Am From
After George Elly Lyon

I am from a long line of tough women who had a sensibility for business, not children.

I am from a lineage of grit, gumption, and grief, trying to improve their station, generation after generation. Pride is devastating.

I am from a canal of shame, pulled to Earth by the trusting freedom of one woman who believed in while staring into the eyes of her lover. The shame cleaved both our hearts.

I am from chaos and disorder, shepherded by grace and unseen forces I call ancestors and angels.

I am from gritty streets, leading to sheets not my own, resting in strangers homes one night then move on.

I am from churches and cathedrals that held my shame, my fears, my secrets. Never doubting my ability to be renewed. My charms reflected in the gentle smile of Mother Mary.

I am from lost and misguided adults adrift on seas of narcotics, misdeeds that spoke of their torments.

I am from the soft forests, carpets of moss that absorbed my sorrows, and loneliness.

I am from growing old too soon and working backward to my youth, as a mother to my own brood.
I am from the sun, a warmth that touches my fervent spirit to no longer living from what I know. To create that which I know not.

I am from his DNA a man I never knew, his hand I held once.

I am from creation herself. No longer lonely for I hold the hand of infinite souls beyond perception leading me deeper into the mystery.

I am from curiosities, undaunted in the darkness, my light illuminates from within. Welcoming intrepid travelers on their discovery.

I am from this world and the next, unconstructed by convention or invention. Consciousness is my magic carpet.

W. 117ᵗʰ there was a knock on the door. My heartbeat quickened, I ran around in a circle, like a trapped animal. I knew Therese was coming to get me, but she never came to the door. Shit, shit, shit. Ok, gather yourself. Everything will be ok.

I slowly unlatch the chain, ever so slowly to help me devise a plan in cas she asks to come in.

"Almost got it, the door lock is a little cranky in her old age," I say. I kept my foot at the base of the door and cracked it just enough to make eye contact. "Good morning! I wasn't expecting you. I'm almost dressed."

"Oh ok," she said. "May I come in and wait for you?"

"Ummm, ahhh, umm. I'll only be a minute. I can meet you in the car."

"Brigid, don't be silly I'm happy to wait inside, it's cold outside."

What Therese didn't know was that it was colder in here. I could let my boss into my apartment that is decorated and presents as a normal situation, but we are hiding. We are hiding the truth of our living environment even from ourselves. Her presence is blowing my cover. I am not ready to accept my reality! *Dammit, why can't she just wait in the car and we can both pretend? I can pretend to have a normal home and she can pretend to keep accepting me as I am.* Which to her looks pretty normal and usual. I keep trying to stall and her insistence is becoming more uncomfortable. I look around one more time, to make sure all the ghosts are back in the closet as best we can muster.

I widen the door and put on my biggest fake smile I can force to my face.

"Good Morning, Therese, thank you for your patience."

"What the hell took you so long? Why were you stalling?"

"Umm, I wasn't stalling, I'm not ready yet." My stomach is churning and I feel a little nauseous.

"Oh, you tree looks nice Brigid. Do you usually leave the lights turned off?" she asks.

"Oh, I haven't plugged them in yet, it's still early." Little does she need to know that our lights have been turned off for weeks.

"Your mom sure likes it chilly in here!"

"Yes, she is a bit of a polar bear. I'll just be one more minute, I need to put on my lipstick." I run to the back of the apartment and throw all my necessities in my bag, and smear on the crimson lipstick, which makes me look piqued. Maybe I just am piqued and am looking for something else to blame it on. Every ounce of my dignity and humility has drained from beneath my porcelain skin. With every drop of saliva I swallow, I am also swallowing down my humiliation. Why am I living like this? What a fraud I am, to walk into one of the most prestigious brokerage firms in Cleveland, and I am destitute.

Buying a pair of stockings to wear with my mandatory dresses is a hardship. And, the irony is that if I am found out and I lose my job, then we won't even have this shell of existence around us. These walls are the only thing keeping me from facing homelessness. I am not sure why that plight seemed graver than my present living circumstances. The walls held great power in helping my sanity remained anchored. This was my 15th Christmas. Ho, ho, ho….

"Therese, thank you for waiting, I am ready." As we drove to the office, she was excitedly rattling off the details for the office Christmas party. This party was meaningful to my wellbeing. I was looking forward to being warm for an extended period of time, as the office closed early, but we were planning to be there well into the night.

The night was the hardest time for me when we were without heat or electricity. In some of our dwellings, you needed one to have another. I acclimated to the obstacles you overcome to live without basic utilities. When the heat is off, sometimes we could use hot plates to warm water for a washing. Other times we could warm beverages to keep our body temperatures from dropping too much. When the lights were out, we would use oil lanterns and candles, they produced their own small amount of heat. But the stillness of the night time I found unnerving. I could hear every creaky noise, the scattering of the critters in the drywall. The night seemed endless and my anxiety would skyrocket.

After all of the festivities and a full belly, Therese offered to take me home after the party, so that I could avoid taking the bus.

I arrived to my Mom sitting alone with the company of candlelight. Our Christmas this year would be bleak, but we still had one another, and for once the gift of her presence was my greatest gift.

Inner Home I have spent my whole life being afraid of what others might think of me. Will they accept me once they know I have a dark side? Am I lovable when I am as unpredictable as a cat in water, swiping my claws upon another? I have a deeply wounded, feral child that lives inside of me. Harmed from a young age, she doesn't trust or know that life can be safe. She doesn't believe my words, only actions. Still suspicious of; love, intimacy, connectedness. Each time I, the big person, allows someone closer to us, closer still, to her—to the vulnerable side of my inner world—she violently rejects these advances and begins spewing venom. Either by pushing people away, saying harsh things, or isolating, I will hide from things that are too threatening, to avoid the wrath that unfolds inside of me. It's a turbulent, fear-ridden place, one that I am trying to know, without expectation or judgment.

My mind drinks this elixir, then pours it back into my cells, blood, and breath. I too begin to believe the venom and lash out. I lurch at the person/s that dare come so close to my tender feral child. Take your acceptance, your high holiness, your enlightenment, and shove it up your ass. This world isn't safe. There is no such thing as unconditional love. I have tried, believe me, I have tried. I have bared my soul to those who inevitably have left me cold and rejected. I have kept quiet, only to have the same outcome. I am tired. My every fiber aches. When will what I am today be enough? When will what I do matter? When will all of my efforts be worth it? Who am I doing this for? Do I even know myself anymore? Am I the child, the adult, the narrator, the director, the abuser, the perp?

When I listen to or read various thought leaders on consciousness, I am confusingly reminded that no one is outside of me. I find it confusing because if I can touch another person and see another person, who isn't acting kindly towards me, am I really alone? I don't think that is their point, as much to say that I am in need of healing or soul growth and these *outside* forces are happening to show me more. Everything I experience is my own projection to help me see myself. Did I rape myself? Did I verbally and physically abuse myself while being high on alcohol and pills? Am I the one who abandoned me time and time again? Then why am I here? How much pain can one person stand, before admitting it's enough? Simple idioms of light, love, and laughter are simple chatter that inflames my intensity. There are pits of shame that keep me from moving. Like a downhill skier with one ski, up and down, side to side, over and over I go this mogul then the next. My heart hangs heavy within me. I shudder to think what would have become of me if not for giving life to our three children. They are the purest mirrors I can see, they give me a breath of hope when all else feels tainted, dark and weary.

Bobo was wheelchair bound and living at what I was told at the time was an assisted living home off of Scranton, just outside of the city. In my later years I came to find out that Bobo was living in public housing, not assisted living. I would visit her often and we would have mini adventures in the neighborhood, also within the home. She would take me to the common area where all of her friends would gather and tell me stories of their lives. I loved sitting amongst the elders hearing tales of what their lives once were, the dreams they still held, and the sorrows they carry.

Bobo gave me two gifts I will always remember; a porcelain doll, and my cat, Mittens. We went together to pick out Mittens. He was at the animal shelter, and we chose one another. Adopting him felt like such a responsible thing to do at that time in my life. I was declaring my promise to care for him on paper, with witnesses!

I called the doll Ginger and she went everywhere with me. She had long curly blonde locks, with a deep royal blue velvet dress, and bonnet. The bonnet may have been my favorite part of her attire. Moving as much as

Faith and I did, I had few possessions, and I was very possessive of my doll. During one of our quick exits, Faith was throwing things into a box and Ginger broke. I remember standing there in disbelief, that Faith was careless and broke the doll that meant everything to me. Especially after saying goodbye to Bobo.

When I was eight years old, almost nine, a tragedy struck which now as a grown woman I am slowly unpacking. The memories of the event itself are fuzzy, but the aftershock still affects me. In that single moment, I made a declaration to the world that I was no longer safe.

Bobo had been in the hospital for a few days. She had diabetes and seldom took her insulin. This time she had a stroke, and her organs were in distress. She died at the hospital. I remember us rushing to the hospital, and my mom was crying. I was confused because I thought we were going to see her. Why was she crying?

The main entrance to the hospital was large and bustling with people. There was a ton of light, and the atmosphere felt rushed. My mom asked me to take a seat, and she would check if I could come to the room. She left me there with her boyfriend, Vince, who I could not stand. He was never a safe person to me and being alone with him added to my anxiety. My mom came back after a few short minutes and told me to stay put; children weren't allowed in the room. She and Vince left, I stayed put. I was so angry—why did he get to see the woman I loved the most? Why was he allowed to be with her, and I wasn't? She didn't even like him! Why was he the one supporting mother?

When we left the hospital and drove home, I overheard a conversation about the severity of my grandmother's health. It looked bleak and left me very fearful. How is this possible? Do people leave you and never come back? My mom always left me, but she would eventually return. I spent most weekends with Bobo, and she always made me feel special. We had a lot of fun together. She was wheelchair-bound most of my youth, but it never slowed her spunk down. There is something about Irish women that they never give up!

That night the phone rang, and it confirmed that my mother and I lost a very special woman in our lives. Although the family stories tell of how mother hated Bobo, and that they were never close, I saw mother's sadness and despair. She was lost like me.

During all of the events for her wake and funeral, I was just passed from car to car, person to person. I wasn't considered or even held during this traumatic time in my life. Everyone was busy with their grief and responsibilities. I needed someone to look me in the eyes and tell me that I will be ok, and that life is safe, that death is a natural part of our cycle. We will all pass away at some point. Instead, they slammed shots of whiskey and told tacky stories of my Bobo. I remember thinking: How strange that they are celebrating her in a bar? Why am I in a bar, drinking a Shirley Temple? I had nothing to celebrate. I was devastated.

The week following her death I stayed shut in my room. I barely ate, spoke or moved. I kept hearing Faith say I was in shock, whatever that meant. I was heartbroken.

She was my person. The pair of eyes that showed me I mattered. That a daisy could lift any heaviness a day may bring. Every time I saw her I felt loved. She looked forward to seeing me, as much as I looked forward to the safety she harbored. She was wheelchair-bound, diabetic, and aged. She faced her life, and I was a second chance. It was hard for Faith, seeing her mother dote on me. I understand now why Faith would leave me at the door, she didn't want the reminders.

I soaked up everything Bobo gave me. With smugness I can't retract. The dark side of pain is it creeps into seemingly simple moments, leaving a residue. I was young. I forgive my ignorance.

I never realized how much this had affected me until last week, on my way to therapy with our daughter. I was feeling so scared and tense, but I couldn't understand why. This wasn't our first appointment. As I tuned into my body and asked what I needed to know, I was taken back to my grandmother's funeral. I remembered feeling unsafe in the world. I never learned to heal that wound, nor did the elders around me. They were hurt, too. It occurred to me that no matter how hard I try to not pass along my wounds, I still have them, and I'm passing them along to our daughter.

She presently doesn't feel safe in the world, either. So I shared with her all that I've shared with you. We agreed that this car ride is helping us both to know that we have one another and can be safe in that knowing. She gently joked that maybe I should take her appointment today; I may need it more than her. That gesture lets me know that the healing has begun.

I will always remember Bobo for her tenderness. Regardless of what others thought of her, she was always kind and considerate of me. Maybe we were both looking for a second try; I at being mothered, her at mothering. We still visit her for Christmas and Mother's Day at Calvary Cemetery. My Aunt Mary taught me the importance of honoring our ancestors, which I am now passing on to our children.

Aunt Mary gave me pictures of Bobo; one was taken on her wedding day. I see much of myself in her eyes. The hope, the cheerful closeness young love brings. She was my Grandfather Stephen's prize. Her beauty was timeless; silky chestnut curls, rosy cheeks, softness in her eyes, slim waist, and long torso. Everyone was in their best form, smiling at the camera. Their life was beginning, and they were prim, stoic, and joyous. Time has a way of wearing down one's smile and glimmers of hope. If you're not careful they're gone, only to be memorialized in the frame.

Nana embodied family; everything about her revolved around family. Making meals, planning get-togethers, every conversation, and expectation, objection— all to foster a close family.

She was the matriarch of Adam's lineage. Born in Ukraine, she came over to Ellis Island in the late 20's and made her way to New York, before moving to Cleveland, Ohio. She lived with her brother (her sponsor to the United States) and his family (a wife and two daughters). She worked at his bar, The Rowley Inn. Eventually, she met and married Alex Lenko, and had one daughter; Ellen (Adam's mother).

The first time I met Nana, we came to her cozy bungalow nestled in a quiet neighborhood just outside of the city. The whole house was perfumed with the scent of pierogis dancing in a pan of butter.

Everything happened around Nana's kitchen table; laughter, tears, memories. I loved her instantly and wished to model her qualities when running my own home. She had few tchotchkes; her home modestly decorated with colorful Ukrainian cross-stitched pillow covers and doilies. A plaque hung in her kitchen that said "Too soon old, too late smart." It summed up her personality. She was a short, stout, and hardy woman. Her hair a soft grey, framing glasses that emphasized her kind eyes. She had a bit of a waddling walk. And her accent was so charming—she always called me Bligid.

Though living with her and our young family was difficult, it also was firm ground. She wanted nothing more than to prep me, mold me into a fine young wife, who knew the importance of family. I knew better and fought her every step of the way...until she was ailing, and I wished to take it all back, and listen. Listen to really soak up the lessons. That time never came.

Adam and I would take time to go to the woods, or take long car rides with Alex. It was a way for us to create a little bit of space when tensions ran high.

She showed me how to cook meals using simple ingredients, with slow cooking times to develop the best flavors. Scrub a floor on your hands and knees, "It's the only way to make sure it's clean." And, to be grateful. Growing up as a child of 13 in a one-room farmhouse, she shared shoes and clothing. If she woke too late, she would be doing house chores, because she didn't have shoes to wear while tending the fields. Her bungalow was her castle, and she appreciated every square inch. It's why I loved her home so much; she filled its entirety with love and appreciation. It took me 14 years to realize that's why it never felt like home after she passed away. I loved her, in the home, never the home itself. There is a difference, and it's a big one. That lesson, perhaps the most important, is what I will remember; that we can be happy anywhere, and to be happy begins with gratitude.

Soon after celebrating her 90th birthday, she had a stroke, then the nursing home, then hospice. The nursing home was a tough stretch to endure during her last days on the planet, we all felt at peace when they transferred her to hospice. It was that time that I held her hand, listened to each wheezing breath, clinging to the hope that she would share one last thought of her wisdom. Something I could remember her by. It turned out that I was able to give that to her. *I whispered in her ear that she i loved, always, will be honored eternally, and is free. We will make it without her, somehow, and thank you. Thank you for helping me to grow as a woman, accepting n into the fold and believing in me. She always did, that is why she gave so much.* She squeezed my hand and passed away a few hours later. It may have been our talk, or maybe not. One can never assume to know the mysteries of life. Being grateful, humble, and present is our best shot at happiness.

Bully Inside Me   I'd like you to meet "Bruce," he is the bully that live inside of me. Bruce used to be the driver of my bus. We were headed on a direct course for being as obnoxious and rude as one could be. Seldom seen to the outside world, Bruce was, however, in full control of me. He would suggest horrible food choices, poor sleeping habits, call me mean names, and showering was completely optional to him.

See, Bruce lived under the delusion that bullying meant being powerful. So he took full advantage of the cozy bunker he found inside of me. He moved in because of a call he received from a very frightened little girl. I was crying out for help, feeling helpless and alone. I needed a friend. Someone who would help me to feel brave, comforted, and protected. Bruce answered and I welcomed him with open arms.

We lived happily together for several decades. Bruce knew his place, which was to keep me motivated. Not too aggressive, but vocal. Bruce loved to be heard, to let people know his opinion of just about anything. I liked the assertiveness Bruce offered. We were a great team.

That was until I began to feel uncomfortable with my edgier side. I was outgrowing the behaviors that once brought me a lot of comfort and satisfaction. Now I was embarrassed by some of the things I said and did, even feeling ashamed of myself at times. I could see that my behavior was uncomfortable for people to be around. Yet I didn't understand why it wouldn't stop. To certain people, no matter how hard I tried, I'd still say rude things.

I took some time away to be with myself and try to understand where this hostility was coming from. Why was I only feeling angry towards certain people? Bruce believed it easier to blame others for my discomforts than allow me the space to learn personal responsibility. If I were to become responsible for my thoughts and feelings, where would he live? As I grew, he shrunk, and moved to the backseat. I regained control of my feelings, my actions, no longer allowing Bruce to bully myself or others. He still comes to visit once in a while—his way of asking if he is still remembered and important to the small child that still lives inside of me.

Bertha I saw her every day, her silky gray hair suspended by her puffy pink rollers of foam, fastened with plastic straps. Wearing her usual attire of oversized white slippers and housecoat (I never knew housecoats came in so many patterns and colors) each morning, she'd lightly step down her stairs and into her grass to retrieve her paper. The delicate way she supported each step left me wondering if I deserved to be held softly by unassuming hands. Age never shadowed her innocence. Her gentleness perfumed our neighborhood. She had been there for decades; everyone knew Bertha. I wondered if she'd still wave hello if she knew that my innocence had been stripped away like the bark of a tree to a starving man.

She waved at me, and her smile washed me clean of my sins. We moved about our lives, curious strangers in a land of familiar faces. Bertha began our friendship at age 84; my first invite came nonchalantly, a suggestion to pop by for lunch one day. She always made egg salad and would leave enough to be shared. I'd never had egg salad until that fresh spring day. As I stepped into her home, I felt the familiarity of my home leave. My eyes soaked up the new sights and sounds of her castle, her walls of safety and refuge.

She had an accent I couldn't place; it was thick, maybe European. It swept over me like a wave of mystery. I believe she knew bits of my story and was too polite to ask. She was there the night the ambulance and police officers left our home. Maybe I was equally mysterious to her. Our lunch was the beginning of an unusual friendship, of two hearts as rare as a four-leaf clover in a meadow. Her home was built in the late 40's, designed by her husband. She raised their children there. Every room shared the same story: loneliness. A house once filled with laughter, busyness, and the comforts of knowing you were necessary, now sat empty. We both were longing to be discovered, to mean something to someone again, to belong.

The castle now echoed of sweet songs from her parakeets, each so happy to have a cage and seeds. Coupled and mated for life, they knew they belonged to each other. I envied their confined bliss. Bertha knew my wing was broken. Though it started as a bump, it had to break to show me I was no longer safe in the world. She never asked me what took place that night. Maybe she was just as afraid to hear the details as my lips were to speak them. She offered me a chance to heal, tending to me as one of her parakeets; filling my belly with seeds of wisdom, letting me rest in her tender hands. She covered my wounds with an unconditional love, when the darkness was my only light.

It's been thirty years since I've thought about her and the castle walls. She knew how to help this broken bird. To open the cage and set me free to fly with an invisible thread that reverberates from heaven to earth. I still belong to her.

Bertha's Refuge living with her negated some bad behavior from Faith. She didn't dare walk into Gramma Bertha's house wreaking of scotch or stumbling. It is one of the reasons I loved living with Bertha. She helped us stay closer to the better versions of ourselves. I swallowed my disgust for Faith's behaviors. Faith tried to be a model mother in front of Bertha.

The rage and disgust I swallowed came out in other ways. In our sleepy neighborhood, many neighbors had lawn ornaments. Little gnomes or pink flamingos (the goose that had seasonal outfits wasn't popular yet). I decided it would be fun to relocate the lawn ornaments to other people's houses. While there, I also stole everyone's hanging flower baskets. This was quite an undertaking and kept me busy, along with a few nameless friends. We hid all of the plants in Bertha's attic. She never went up there, and I tucked everything away in a few cubbies. It was such a rush doing it the first night, that we continued doing it for a few weeks. The neighbors found this assault on their yard decor intolerable and called a community meeting. They wanted to begin a crime watch to catch the criminals at large. Faith and Bertha had their feathers ruffled as well and marched to the meeting along with all of our neighbors. I hid. I couldn't believe that my misdeeds created such an upheaval. It never occurred to me that I was a vandal.

My anger and discontent about my life created a shit storm! When they came home from the meeting, Faith marched right up to me.

"Where are the plants?!"

"What are you talking about?"

"Brigid cut the crap. I know it's you and those hooligans from down the street."

"What do you mean it's us?"

"The whole community knows it's you! We are the only house to not have any of our decorations stolen! It doesn't take a detective to figure out that my daughter is the culprit."

Ooooh boy! I pleaded and danced around the topic far longer than I should have because now she was screaming. Faith did many things, but she reserved screaming for something really bad. I, with a slumped head and heart filled with shame, took her to my hiding space in the attic. She was floored. It was packed to the ceiling with dead houseplants and yard ornaments.

"Why did you do this?! Do you know that I have to repay every single person in order to keep you from going to juvie?!"

"What's juvie?"

"It's a jail for children. The police were there tonight and said that if the responsible party doesn't make amends, they will be taken to jail. How could you do this? I am so ashamed of you."

Welcome to the club, Faith. I have the same opinion of you.

High School Guidance Counselor I apologize for not remembering your name—time has a way of stripping away details. I am now forty-four years old, mother of three, and married for seventeen years. Are you surprised? I would never have guessed this fate all those years ago, that time in my life when you knew the details of me intimately. It's funny how time has a way of moving people in and out of our lives. I want you to know that although some of the layers have washed away, the key you held in my heart is still hanging in stillness. You were a pivotal person in my life. You may not know how much you gave to me. Maybe you do, and you gave it without any expectations. I feel it's important for me to share with others the role you had in my life, and how you changed the direction I was heading.

We met junior year of high school. I was spinning out of control, drinking, skipping school, although outwardly I appeared just fine. When we first met, I recall feeling uneasy because you could see deeper than most. You weren't afraid to see into my fears. You were willing to sit in the discomforts with me. So we sat quietly for our first few meetings. You were assigned my case because I needed to get on track for graduation, and college. You were to be my guide. Little did I know that you were a gift, sent to guide my future in a way that had very little to do with academia!

As the weeks clicked on we began to cultivate a friendship. I allowed you to peer into my pains and understand the difficulties I was facing. I had to work a part-time job daily to afford to live. I had a mother who was checked out, and who wasn't able to guide me. I shared of the abuse I had experienced, and the constant fears that whirled around me. You never flinched, you never wavered. You sat in the pits of my pain with me, just as children would sit in a sandbox. No expectations, only discovery. There came a time when I looked forward to our visits, and to have your safety.

Your presence was always enough for me, the way you listened was like syrup on my wounded heart. I had never been heard in that way.

I remember you had an extra ticket to Swan Lake. I can still recall the excitement I saw in you, to offer the ticket to me. The chance to experience the beauty of the theater. The performance was breathtaking! I'd never been exposed to anything like it, and since then I have become an avid lover of the theater, ballet, and anything in performing arts.

Afterward, you surprised me again, by thanking me for accompanying you! I will never forget that feeling of being appreciated for my company. You answered to my inner need to be special, to be valued. Wherever you are in your life, may you know that you stopped me from my path of self-destruction and self-abuse? It may have been a few years later that I can credit you for this turnabout. I still struggled with substance abuse and neglect of my body. But the seeds you planted began to sprout. Little by little I remembered my specialness, that I am of value, and I needed to treat myself as such. Today I am still healing from what I endured as a child, however, my love of self, art, and connection continue to bloom and expand in my world, and in those I love. Thank you for being so kind and willing to nurture the qualities in my being I wasn't aware lived there.

Money One way we worked to secure rent was selling roses. We would wake early in the morning and begin sorting flowers for arrangements. I would help Faith prepare several buckets worth. I always enjoyed taking a mixture of things and combining them to make something beautiful. Mixing the roses with carnations seems an unlikely choice, but if you shorten the stem of the carnation, it is a lovely accent to the star, rose. Roses always hold a prominence. A certain air of: *Look at me. I stand tall and erect to be noticed.* Carnations are more of the spirited sort. They like to mingle and snuggle while standing on their own texturally. And Baby's Breath; so delicate, gentile, and pushy. There's so many of them to one branch it's like inviting a gang of hungry pups; no order or purpose, just pushing and shoving until they all get a place around the tit. Who can blame them—they're soft and sweet and demand their place amongst the bouquet.

We would load her Gremlin and head out just after sunrise to find the best spot. It didn't matter if it were raining, cold, or blazing hot—we wer there. I always noticed that no matter the reason why the person decided to buy a bouquet, it was sure to bring another pleasure. That is the gift o flowers, they lighten any story.

Most likely the most humorous job we tried on was passing out phone books. It seemed harmless; easy and sensible. We teamed up with a friend of Faith's who drove a station wagon. The bright blue beauty sparkled an gleaned. Little did the car know what she was about to endure! The idea i that the more we could load and distribute, the more money everyone stood to make. We loaded the wagon taking extra precautions to utilize every square inch of space. Stepping back, proud of our efforts, only to notice the one shortcoming: no one had anticipated the weight of the books. The wagon was touching the ground in the rear! There was no wa to drive the car.

Kelli waking up to the sound of the oil lamp trickling, my head hurts and I am a bit disoriented as to where I am. As I lay there looking around, I begin to notice that everything is, in fact, familiar. The oil lamp is past the bed to the left. The lava lamp is also bubbling and gurgling on the desk beside me. There are clothes strewn about and the comforter is Kelli's. I look to my right and she is there sleeping. As I roused myself from the bed, feeling dizzy and very thirsty, I am awash with shame. This is how the last three years have felt. Countless nights of sacrificing my dignity because I knew no other way. I am sleeping with a girl who is four years my senior, and the daughter of Faith's good friend. I'm not sure how they would have identified themselves with one another. I know they liked to party together. That is how Kelli and I met. A few years earlier I was still living in the house with no soul and her mom was a friend of the homeowner, Uncle Cole, Faith may have known her before that, but it's the first time I can recall seeing Kelli. Our moms would insist we hang around one another since we were the only children.

I looked up to Kelli. She was confident, smart, pretty, and bold. She never had a hard time telling someone how she felt, or what she wanted. I was still timid and tried to have a low line of visibility. When I moved in with Bertha, Kelli was allowed to spend the night. That's when things between us began developing into more exploration than what I assumed most kids were doing at sleepovers. One night, we were sharing the bathtub. Why this was normal to Bertha, I will never know. I was quite nervous about it, as being seen without clothes on was threatening for me. I wasn't comfortable with my body or my body being exposed. As we sat in the tub, she suggested we play a game where we show one another our parts. My stomach hurt so badly, as I wanted to be her friend, and for her to think I was cool and not a scaredy cat. But I didn't want to play this game.

My body and mind were still very hurt by the man that snuck into my room. I didn't want anyone to touch me. I also was unable to find my scream or ability to say no. I was trapped. I went along with her game and kept playing it for several years. It became normal for her to make suggestions and me to go along with them. She was good at getting what she wanted from me. I was good at playing along. I was so confused by all of it. I only wanted a friend, someone that I could trust and know that they were looking out for me. The touching, penetration and endless fondling left me whirling in confusion. My body eventually craved our time together. My mind never agreed that there was consent or pleasure in our encounters. I never knew if she was in love with me, if I was in love with her, or this was all a game. There are never two winners of the same game.

We would do things that most tweens and teens do; roller skating, dancing, movies. She had a rather large circle of friends that she introduced me to. I was the joke among most of the boys, as she was always the one they were interested in. I was "too fat, too round, too young, and too awkward." Being fat was, in some ways, a blessing, though in middle school I would find it a curse. Being fat or overweight in the late 80's was worse than having a disease. No boys wanted to be known as the guy who dates "fat girls." All the boys that Kelli knew tolerated me or made fun of me. She was the shapely one that they wanted to be closer to.

No matter how many times I told Faith, "No, I don't want to see Kelli," I would soon be dropped off there. There were no cell phones or easy ways to get a ride home. I would need a quarter and way to sneak out if I wanted to get picked back up. The other way was to go with Kelli when she wanted to party and get drunk. I was around age 11/12. If I called Faith drunk she would rush right over. This was easier than taking the bus home late at night. The older I got, the more I became aware that the things going on between us were not loving or safe. She was in need, and I could no longer be the one giving to her. I wasn't safe.

One night we were out with her male friends. These guys had a car which was usually loaded with pot, beer, and cigarettes. As we went driving around with them, they were passing around a joint. She kept insisting that I smoke it. I had only smoked pot a few times before and I didn't like it. I declined, and she insisted. We went round robin for a few minutes until, finally, I gave in. I took a hit and it tasted awful, everyone in the car was laughing at me because I was hacking and drooling.

We made it to a party and the next thing I remember was Faith getting me into her car. I was a mess; lying propped up against a building (I think they dumped me and called Faith), vomiting, rambling, in and out of consciousness. She was screaming at me, as I came in and out she was speaking of how careless I was and didn't I want to live? Why would I ever say ok to a party with all the older boys, who had drugs? What was I thinking?!

The joint was laced with embalming fluid! Little did she know that the boys weren't the threat, it was Kelli. This stint had me grounded for weeks and that began the distance between us. I kept pulling farther and farther away.

My dignity slowly came back to me the farther away I got from her. My sexuality was stunted and damaged. In my late teens, friends who I entrusted this information with told me I was a lesbian. I wasn't attracted to women. I was always attracted to men. "Oh, that's simple, you're bisexual." I didn't feel that was true either.

Even though, I told boys I had been with a girl, for attention. They seemed to like the idea of that, and it helped my pudgy self to be seen. I don't feel good about the lies I told to get noticed. I again wanted someone to love me, to belong somewhere. I wanted to believe that the more I gave the more assurances I would always be wanted and belonged.

We remained acquaintances into my late teens. She met a man who I introduced her to, they married, and I was her maid of honor. I know she had children but what became of her, I don't know. That time in my life still hangs over me with a grimy feel of confusion, distortion, things left unsaid. I have forgiven her, myself, the air between us. We were both trying to learn about life on the edge. Neither one of us had a steady home life at the time. We looked into one another to learn, feel comforted and seen. She was there for me the best way she could be.

Swing Set was gifted to us twelve years ago by my mother-in-law Ellen's neighbor. *Ellen was direct competition to Faith in our budding relationship. She was and still is considerate of me. She listens when I speak and we can go anywhere in our conversations. She feeds the part of me that was abandoned by Faith. I am not a threat to Ellen; my thoughts aren't jeopardizing to her. I am thankful for the many years we have spent in relationship, learning about the roles of mother and daughter even if somewhat through association, then birth.* I was pregnant with Michael when we brought it home. I spent hours sanding, priming and restoring its luster, excited to give our children something I hadn't grown up with; a yard, a fence, and a mother who was home every day.

Countless children played in our yard (some now adults away at college, or beginning their careers) on summer days, laughs abounding. We kept upping our creativity with new ways to enjoy the same old swing set.

Hose tied to the slide. Put said slide into the opening of *the pool, Nichol and I found at a garage sale and tied onto the roof of her car, because she loves me, and we had just enough rope to make it happen!*

Year after year the swing set was a daily activity I shared with our children, their friends, and the moms of their friends. So many memories attached to the cold metal. Now a new family came to give rise to new memories.

Saying goodbye was hard. I hadn't fully realized how much the neighbor had gifted us! It wasn't just a swing set, it was a reason to gather and create memories.

The new creator of memories is a little girl, two years old, curls that bounce, eyes that twinkle, a giggle that lingers.

Integrity the chinks in my mortar were from the countless times I sacrificed my integrity for a momentary sense of belonging or fitting in. Too many times I stayed longer then I should have with boys that weren' good for me, or groups that only used me for their amusement. The loneliness I felt was oppressively uncomfortable, I would do close to anything to be accepted into a group. The young men I met through various groups would only find me attractive if they were alone or under the influence of some substance. I was not the chosen girl by anyone until Christian. He chose me, from the start. We met when I was a freshman in High School, a mutual girl we knew, Janice, introduced us. I had run into her at a party, she was a girl I knew from Mortimer. Christian and I attended St. Philip and James together. Though I didn't remember him, he remembered me from second grade! He said we were in the same class together. He remembered me! I was memorable; this is why the guy broke my heart. He was the first male figure in my life who didn't TAKE from me; he gave, until his time for giving to me ended. The wound he left no longer aches, as he was the guide I used when marrying Adam. Christian gave me an irreplaceable gift; he showed me what it felt like to be treasured and belong. To him I was always enough. The memory of our young romance was the metric I used to find the right man for me to marry. I didn't settle. I selected.

No matter what our circumstances, Faith and I always found shelter. Even if one of us was in jeopardy, it seemed a better choice than homelessness. If I had a say in those early years, I would have chosen just the two of us. Even in her most desperate states, she was always my home. She wasn't a physically affectionate woman. What I always longed for was to be swooped up, stroked, looked at and assured it would all be ok. That she was protecting me and we would make it, tomorrow wouldn't be as hard as today. Eventually, when that became our reality, it didn't feel as sweet as I'd always dreamed. When she finally gave up drinking, I was too bitter to notice. We moved after finding our apartment completely cleaned out by James. It was his last jab at Faith, some attempt to have control or the final say. What he didn't know was the biggest blow he gave wasn't physical; he destroyed her illusion of home and family. In my own heart, we were never a family.

Looking back, I believe that is why she wouldn't even entertain the idea that James was fondling me in my sleep. To admit anything was awry would destroy the facade she had built. Having a home meant something to Faith; she spent our entire lives trying to secure a permanent home, trying to fill it with memories and people she cared for. It was a fantasy that only she conjured for herself, her sanity, her peace. I no longer blame her; I have forgiven both of them, repeatedly. I started small and move to the bigger hurts. Now I understand, being a mother to our three children, that home will never be the place we live. It's the space we keep in one another's hearts. That's why you can move, lose, chase, destroy, and keep rebuilding. The strength of the human heart is the greatest foundation for which to build a home.

The Learning House

Our home
Our body
Our occupations
Our relationships
Our child/ren
They are all a learning house
Unique textures, veneers
How is one to know how to care
Tend
Sweep
Adorn
Anything that they've never been responsible for
How is one to know the holes never leave the door
Paint peels
Hearts break
Bodies expand and contract
How is one to know what is at stake
It is all a learning house
Important indeed
Suffering from scuffing the walls
A choice
Not a need
It is all a learning house
A time to root
Weed
Lead with curiosity
There is no permanence
It is all a learning house
Children know this from the start
If we took their lead
Living lighter in heart
It is time to refresh
Restore
Be reverent
Explore
And Enjoy
The learning house in which you dwell

One doesn't become an expert through theory, but experience...

Chapter Seven
Emboldened Mothering

I t wasn't until I became a mother that I understood why people say that life is hard. Adam and I were young, vibrant, healthy, and financially stable. We had plenty of time and energy for everything we wanted to try. We traveled, read, slept late, and stayed out until the wee hours of the morning. We literally had nothing to be responsible for but ourselves.

Ah, and then the children came. I revolted at the notion that a little child came with so many responsibilities. How could they need all of these clothes, toys, and things? Yet, there I stood in the nursery of our first born, with more things than I knew what to do with. All of them from a place of I love. I was scared. Scared to say no to the things I was told I needed. Scared to listen to myself. Scared to listen to Adam. Scared. So very scared.

After Alex's delivery, during one of my nurse follow-ups, she suggested I speak with my midwife about my feelings. I cried all of the time. I could barely get out of bed to dress or care for myself and I was home alone with a newborn, which in and of itself was scary. Babies do not come with a manual, and when you are breastfeeding, keeping track of the feedings, his poops, and how often he was peeing, was ridiculous. I was convinced that I would be the only mother in the universe whose swollen boob would turn out to be a dud!

Well, on this particular day, I may have proven myself right. Alex was screaming, I kept putting him to my breast, and he would scream at it. I was perplexed and stressed. So I sat down and tried to calm down, with a screaming baby. You can see where this is going. I put him in his crib and called Adam.

"Honey, it's bad. My boob is huge, the baby is screaming and I can't figure out what to do. He isn't wet, he just slept, he yells at my boob. Please help me!"

Adam, always logical; "Did you feed him?"

"Honey, I tried, he just screamed at my breast."

"Brigid, do you remember in our feeding class, how they mentioned engorgement?"

"No, what the hell is that?"

"It's you, honey, I will be right there."

Adam came into the apartment with two different types of breast pumps. They were glowing like angels! My boobs, by this time, were so big and swollen. Alex could not be soothed, and I was a mass of nerves! Finally, after working the pump, I felt relief and was able to get him latched on and fed. While being engorged, I also couldn't sit on the toilet without the pillow they provided as I was cut from front to back during his delivery. I was losing a lot of blood and was pale as a ghost. I felt like shit almost every day. An incapable shit, who was now responsible to care for a helpless baby.

I and postpartum depression became besties. I begrudgingly took the medication, which was supposed to help me feel better, except I didn't feel good about taking the medication. I felt like a failure—that I couldn't even have a baby without screwing it up. I didn't understand all that was actually taking place within my body. I experienced a trauma. Alex getting stuck in the canal was, in fact, a trauma to both of us. A level four episiotomy is another trauma, coupled with the natural fluxes of hormones and adjustments. It was a lot to take in all at once. I had never cared for babies when I was growing up. All people should be responsible for a baby in their younger life, all people! I had zero framework to work off of, except for feeling lousy, and being depressed and scared out of my mind. Did I mention we lived alone in Kent, Ohio? And, Adam worked two jobs to keep us fed and housed!

Life wasn't ideal. This wasn't the happy dream world I had envisioned while watching all of the T.V. shows about having a baby. PPD did, however, teach me a few things that I may not have found otherwise. I learned to ask for help. I learned to be seen in my vulnerability. I learned that it isn't my capacity to do it all. I learned that it is ok to be afraid, and not know. And that nothing lasts forever. It was a moment in time, not a sentence.

I've yelled at them, let them cry it out (not long, but we tried it). I was distant and lost in my depression. I can think back to so many memories of looking into their eyes and thinking to myself, *why, why did you choose me? I am a mess and not suited for you in this lifetime. Why did you choose me?*

I was the "never" mom. "I will never let my children eat sugar." "I will never let my children watch T.V." "I will never yell at my children." "I will never ignore my children like my mother did." I think I did all of it on the same day; loaded them up on sugar while watching T.V., as I screamed at them to stop watching so much T.V. and then ignored their efforts to connect.

I didn't know what I was doing. I only knew that I wanted them to have the best, but I didn't believe it came from me. Not knowing that by simply being me, it would be enough. It would, in fact, be more than they needed. I simply didn't know. I trusted that the magazines knew what was best for my family. I listened intently to everyone around me and their perspective. *Surely these are wise people I have surrounded myself with. They must know more than me.* Yet, we were all new moms. Did we really know more than the next? Who is to say? It's all a trial of learning. I could spend the rest of my life beating myself up, for not being kind, gentle, soft, available, and trustworthy. I could, but where would that get me? What would that help in my children's memories? If I want to be an empowered woman, I will learn to own my faults. I will apologize and learn. I will grow. I will say I am sorry to myself, too. I will forgive myself. I have forgiven some, not everything. I am still working on that piece. I pray that our children have forgiven me. That one day they will look back on their childhoods and feel warmth within the memories. A place that will remind them that this simple woman (me) tried her best and often had their best interests in her heart. She wasn't always an impatient, spasmodic, unpredictable woman. That there were those moments where time slowed, smiles glowed and laughs were imprinted.

My history left me with much insecurity about mothering my own brood. When Adam and I met, I was convinced I would never bring a child into the world. I had my reasons—overpopulation, emotional immaturity, financial instability—none of these were the core reason. The core was that I was afraid of bringing a child into the world and disappointing him or her by being a below-average parent. How was I supposed to raise a child when I never was one? From as far back as I can recall I was the mother to Faith; worrying about her needs health, wellbeing, meals, and jobs. Somehow being her caregiver never registered to me as the same level of responsibility as being a parent. Adam was eager to be a father and wouldn't hear of my reasons for wanting to abstain.

We had celebrated Ellen's (Adam's mother) birthday over the weekend and for the two days preceding I was deathly ill. I couldn't smoke a cigarette, eat, or drink anything without vomiting. When I returned to work I asked my friend and colleague to go with me to get a pregnancy test at lunch. She laughed and thought it was silly of me to spend our time this way. I kept having a nagging feeling that I might be pregnant. I had never felt this ill before and everything in my body tingled and ached at the same time. We hurried to the drugstore, nervously giggling. Half apprehension, half anticipation! Got back to the office, went into the stall and wetted the moisture strip. Those were the longest two minutes of my life. Lisa and I anxiously waited, giggling, sighing, and pacing. The timer went off and sure enough two blue crosses! I was pregnant. My initial reaction wasn't glee or excitement, it was a terror. I began sobbing and saying all of my fears. *I can't do this. I don't want to do this. I simply can't be a mother. I am not made for this.* She grabbed me and gave me the biggest hug of my life. I called Adam as I couldn't possibly wait until after work. I was so angry with him. He had one job to do and that was to NOT get me pregnant. How could he possibly make this choice for both of us? I wasn't on birth control or insisting on condoms. It was equally my responsibility to protect myself if I was certain to never have children. There was a subconscious part of me that wanted this experience.

Alex was our first. He was my saving grace. I gave up smoking, began to care about what I ate, and hydrated. I fell in love with water and spinach. remember Faith telling me that she would consume crazy amounts of chicken salad while pregnant with me. I thought it remarkable that I didn like chicken salad at all in adult life. I must have been filled up for this lifetime!

Three children later and we are done having children. Michael was our last and I had my tubes tied during his delivery. He was delivered via C-section, which made the decision to have them tied easier. I fought hard verbally and emotionally to not be a mother, yet, when my tubes were tied, I was fighting to remain necessary in some way. I felt a primal part of me was cut away. My role, my right, my viability all snipped at that moment. I would never have foreseen such a reaction. I mourned that decision for a solid year. Not only was it physically hard to forget, the emotional piece was most difficult to sit with. I wasn't trained at this time on how to deal with my emotions. I had two emotions, sad and angry— another reason why I felt inept at raising children.

Faith came to dinner on St. Patrick's Day, this was our tradition. No matter where either of us were, we would always meet for St. Patrick's Day corned beef and cabbage. This was our reunion dinner, as I had cut Faith out of my life for two years leading up to this day. We invited her to our home at Adam's urging to celebrate. Adam and I found out that we were expecting, the sex unknown, and were excited to share the news. Faith told me, "It's going to be a boy and he will be good to you."

The day of the delivery I had to have a spinal and be prepped for surgery because the baby was so big that they weren't comfortable with me attempting natural childbirth, especially with my history of Alex getting stuck in the canal. During the delivery, I remember them cutting me to get the baby and then I was alone, the room was distant, cold, and very bright.

Faith was standing to my right and she kept saying to me, "This isn't your time, get back in your body; this isn't your time get back in there!"

I came back into the room and Adam was to my left rubbing my head and calling my name. "Brigid breathe! Breathe! You're turning blue" There were beeps and alarms going off. I was back with Faith.

"Brigid, I died so that I could keep you alive, get back in there. It's not your time to die."

I heard Adam telling me they had to rush the baby to NICU, because "his" breathing wasn't going well. We had a boy!

I saw Faith one last time, thought it would be several years later that I acknowledged her for the best gift she could ever give me. We were celebrating my fortieth birthday in a rented cabin deep in the Hocking Hills; the lavish home was suited for royalty! As we sat around the fire that night telling stories, watching the embers dance in the air; I was back in the delivery room, remembering the whole event. As shivers covered my body, I silently thanked Faith for giving me a second chance. For all that we had been through; her helping me stay with my body made it all worth it. It wasn't my time and I still had work to do here. Her death was our redemption.

The Children

When I worry about parenting children in times like these
That my children may not have clean water
Untainted food
Clean Soil
Pure air to breathe

I see the way they notice the trees and lakes
With gentle hands and revere

When I worry that my children aren't being seen
Told what to do instead of encouraged
Fitting a mold
Not free to express their soul

I see the ways they stand in their power
With a compassionate "No, that's not right for me."

When I worry that they may never see the world with peace
Unconditional love
Prosperity for all

I see the way they save pennies to pass out to the homeless
Being frugal in their requests because others have less

When I worry that I am not a good enough mother
Passing along my shadows
Unconscious habits

I see the way they remind me of what is right
That I am just as lovable in my darkness, as my light
Lending a hand when the world feels heavy and sad

When I worry that they may lose their freedom to travel the world
Explore and spread their wings

I see the way they hold their dreams
Assured and confident that the world will come to its senses
No longer in need of refugee camps or fences

When I worry that they play too many video games
Not reading enough books
Or have yet learned how to cook
I see the way they grab me to look at the sky
See all the stars
Or glow of a sunrise

When I worry that I haven't taught them well
Beyond how to spell or cross their T's
Understanding consideration
Active listening

I see the way they are learning to engage
Without being hasty or curt
Sitting with another and holding their hurt

When I worry that the days are going too fast
We haven't spent enough time together
Some memories feeling farther away

I see the way they're laughing, playing, being themselves today
Talking and sharing away
And when the sun begins to set
They snuggle in close for one more minute

Watching the car go down the driveway was crushing. Firstly, he drove off in our only car, my car. A powder blue Honda Accord I had purchased on my own when we had broken off our engagement the first time.

I was so pissed that I was being left with Nana and two very young children. *Why does he get to run off?* Though I wasn't surprised, I was surprised. Adam banks his whole character on one quality; loyalty. Where the hell was his loyalty now?

Being a stay at home mom, I was with Nana all the time and we weren't acclimated to sharing a home well. Everything I did was in question. The way I washed dishes: she preferred to let the water run the whole load, I liked to fill the sink and wash them, and then rinse them. She would tell me I was wasting too much water doing it my way.

I wasn't allowed to mop the floor with a stand-up mop. *"The only way to get a floor clean is on your hand and knees."* The best part, she would watch over me when I did it. It drove me crazy! Trying to keep a tidy house—or did I mention that it was a tiny small house, the total square footage 999 that included a partially finished basement. Adam and I had always lived in small spaces. Just the two of us—this was a whole new level of adjustment! The kids were sleeping in our room until we got the spare room set up for Alex. Mae stayed in the crib in our room when we moved Alex. Everything was tense. It wasn't Nana's fault. I was a boiling pot; my life was hard at the time. Being pregnant and high risk was enough, but we were dealing with relocating, Adam being out of work, a young son, and Faith. Everyone had needs! Especially me, I needed Adam to lift some of the burdens for me, not become one of them.

I wasn't ready to say goodbye. There were countless questions unanswered. I was so green, lost in the mystery of how I can wade through these waters. My mother wasn't perfect, yet she had experience. She had years ahead of me in living. I was desperate to know there's hope. That postpartum depression would pass. The feelings of extreme isolation and loneliness would lift. Assured somehow that the children wouldn't be harmed by my ignorance and follies. She was gone and I was left to discover life without her. I read countless books. Went to classes, therapy, more classes, and more therapy. I was so convinced that I couldn't be a good mother that I was overlooking all of the ways I was doing it well.

I began to ease my thoughts about what a good mother looked like, and spent more time paying attention to how it felt to be a mother.

Was I connecting with our children?

Did I understand their needs?

Was I present for the unexpected conversations or snuggles?

These basics are the foundation of our relationship. Nothing matters if I am not tending to the basics. As I slowly matured and let go of the grasping notion that my mother was the only anchor I had in my life, I slowly began to make new relationships that helped me to feel less isolated. I joined groups for families that would hold regular outings for us. Little by little, I was exposing myself to being vulnerable to other mothers. What I noticed is that most of us had the same insecurities. The idea of perfection is laughable, so laugh! Just as a bloom begins to slowly unfurl, I too was opening my closed off heart, learning to trust life and the direction it was leading me.

There are times in my life when I just know that something's going to come to fruition. I was slowly awakening and thirsting for some type of Soul Food. I began watching Oprah Winfrey's Life class pretty regularly on Sunday nights. I remember sitting there one night thinking that someday in my life I would be on that stage. Why the thought came to me, I do not know, but it was very clear, just as the night I professed that I would have my works of art hanging in a local Gallery in Lakewood Ohio. Several years later, after immense dedicated exploration of my craft, I stepped into the same gallery I had walked past night after night, met the owner and three months later my photographs were on exhibit! Again, why I knew that this would take place, I don't know, but that little whisper that lives inside of me, I call her hope. She is the same hope that I had as a little girl growing up in chaos, disconnect, and scarcity. Every night I would go to bed with a sad or scared heart. With yelling in the background, or Faith lost in her addiction, I would talk with hope and she would assure me that tomorrow would be a better day, and most of the time she was right. I built a strong relationship with hope, learned to trust that even if I didn't understand or know how something would come to be, she was wiser than me, and would show me the way.

As I stepped through the doors of Harpo Studios holding Adam's hand, I knew that hope was right alongside us. She had led the way for this moment to come into being. It all seemed so innocent; I filled out an online essay on Oprah's Facebook page. Though I can't recall the exact prompt, there were numerous questions asking questions like; *why do I have insecurities as a parent? What I would be willing to do to break free from these insecurities?* In the essay, I wrote about my childhood and feeling that I wa left without a roadmap. I'm not like the other women who just know how to be a Mom. I am somehow flawed or at a disadvantage because Faith didn't raise me in society's white picket fence.

Forgetting all about the essay, months later I received a phone call from a 312 area code, which I knew was Chicago. At first, I thought it must have been some type of solicitor. Later I listened to the voicemail and learned it was one of Oprah's producers calling to do a phone interview with me and my family, to see if we would be a good fit for her upcoming Life class on Conscious Parenting. The hardest part of the entire experience was the phone interview. We knew if we said yes, we would be exposing the tenderest and vulnerable parts about ourselves publicly. To my surprise, our children said they would do it, and Adam also agreed. After several hours of questions, they invited us to come to Chicago, all-expenses-paid. Adam and I loaded up the car a few weeks later bound for Chicago!

The children weren't invited along because they had enough children participating. Our entire ride there we were bursting with the excitement of what this experience would possibly be like, how could we even know?! When we arrived at the studio, they took us into the Green Room which was quite beautiful, though not green. It was large and every wall had a poster-sized photo of Oprah and a famous guest. There were cream-colored chairs lining the center of the room, and a few along the outer walls. On one side of the room was the makeup artist stations, chairs, and lights. The makeup crew came out and fluffed us and primped us.

I think there were approximately 18 parents partnered, or not, that were a part of this experience. We had a guided tour of Oprah's old studio where she filmed her show for decades. Then they took us onto the Life class stage and I had this overwhelming sense of standing amongst greats. Being an avid fan of the Oprah show, I knew she had interviewed some of the top thought leaders of our world. Here I was, a suburban housewife from Cleveland, Ohio, standing on the same stage, looking pretty fly I have to say.

As we sat there waiting for everyone to get situated, I could feel the nervous energy amongst all of us. I asked the set producer if we could do a round or two of Om chants to help sync our energy. Everyone on the stage agreed and I led a few rounds. When we opened our eyes, Oprah Winfrey and Dr. Shefali Tsabary, the author of *The Conscious Parent*, were standing in front of us with large smiles.

As we began filming, my nerves settled, and I listened to each of the participant's stories with rapt attention. We all share similar struggles, they may have a different flavor, but in the end, we are all trying to figure this out. We all question how to raise children to be well balanced, when inside we are scared! I was in awe of each person's courage, their intense devotion and love for their family.

Adam and I had pizza that night afterwards. My purse was filled with sandwiches that were left over from the day's taping. As we walked to Giordano's in Chicago, we encountered several homeless people. I offered them sandwiches and smiles, light conversations about their day, how they were feeling. Adam was slightly uncomfortable with this. I'd been doing street outreach in Cleveland for a little over a year and was used to this type of spur of the moment interaction.

We made our way to dinner and were still buzzing with excitement over our day. We met Oprah, I learned how to "Tweet", we met amazing people and had many laughs. It was a very uplifting time in our relationship. We felt hopeful about parenting again. We could see that there was a possibility for two people with different ideology to come to together and raise their children consciously. I felt so proud of him for making this trip and agreeing to be on the show, for supporting me, and being open to the unknown. We were on national television sharing our parenting struggles! We were so brave.

When I stepped out of Harpo studios, I stood on the sidewalk and declared to the Universe that I would be back sitting on stage with Oprah, not as a participant, but as her guest speaker. Speaker of what? That was irrelevant; I once again had that inkling of knowing someday I would be there again.

We returned home and settled back into the routine of our lives, we made a new commitment to be on the same page as parents. That is one of our biggest struggles, as I am eager to implement conscious parenting principles and Adam is disbelieving and wants to use the model he was raised with, which is more authoritarian. We have used this model and I am not seeing a result of it having positive outcomes. Our children are resentful of our strong handed approach. They don't feel seen or heard when we are "laying down the law," or "do as we say, not as we do." It's something that doesn't sit well with me, and yet, back to the insecurities. I didn't have a strong model of how to discipline and set boundaries. I ran the roost growing up.

Adam's sense of trust in me with the children is strained at best. He finds me to be passive and too obliging. I find it to be connected and spacious to understand their emotions, even if "bad" they are communicating and it's helpful to understand what they are communicating, instead of shutting it down. I'm not saying I am perfect, far from it. I do have more interest in understanding where our children are at.

My approach not only irritates Adam but also Mae. She finds me to be most annoying and irritating. She is also my shadow hunter. She sees all of the ways I contradict myself, how I am hypocritical and intolerant. Both parts of me are true. I am building balance with what I knew and what I find as the desired outcome. It takes time to build something you've never had.

One of my mentors lends a motherly nurturing energy for my inner child. My inner child (Feral Child) scurries at any type of loving compassion, yet it's what she craves most. Remembering all the times I mothered Faith, I realize that learning how to be a mom wasn't the hard part. What has been hard is learning how to take care of myself, learning how to be my own parent, with compassion, kindness, and nurturing. This is something I give, but it's from a place of practicing, not embodiment. That is why it feels disingenuous when I offer it to myself, because there is nowhere for it to land within. I still have layers of armor around my dear Feral Child's heart.

Mae has been my teacher on learning how to parent myself, as I had to quickly adapt to the turmoil that was taking place in our relationship. This adaptation didn't come from a place of survival, but a deep longing to know that we would both be ok. That everything will make sense in due time, and for right now be present—as present as ever—and allow it to be what it is. I was learning how to build a relationship with myself and beginning to mother myself as I was assisting her process. I wasn't parenting her. I was witnessing.

My heart is raw, I am standing on new earth. It's still settling from being tilled and turned. This place, while mildly familiar, is unsteady. I wish to dig myself into this earth and hide. Hide from my bigger self that is emerging. Hide from the sorrow and shame of being this bigger version of me. I have no framework for how to carry this bigger self. It no longer stands erect on my tired legs. Like a baby deer being born, I am clumsy, wobbly, and overjoyed to be out. To be here, drying and curing, so that I can sprint. This phase, while new, isn't foreign. I have done this countless times in my life. Never by conscious choice. Never by repeated vocalization. I am claiming my right to be known.

Letting my fears ride shotgun, I am here letting the world know that I am worthy of being known. Giving from a place of certainty, not wonder. Not stymied effort. This is one hundred percent conscious effort. It's not hard, it's consistent. The hard part was saying yes to being conscious. You know the famous scene in the Matrix when Theo (the prodigy) has to choose between the red or the blue pill? Taking the pill is the hard part. Subsequently, everything that follows is new, disorienting, and scary. Scary because, until that moment, I hadn't made a choice in my life that I was aware of for my benefit. I had been making choices that met someone else's expectation, need or opinion of me. Swallowing that pill, waking up. That was the hardest part. Because I had no way of knowing anything that was to follow. No way out. Only through.

I have been a part of a women's empowerment circle for almost a year. Last night I opened my vulnerability full throttle and some of my sisters found my sharing a bit overwhelming. I found that I was being compared to and was receiving flippant remarks. I called each of them on it and shared from the place of how their choice affected me. In the past, I would have swallowed my feelings and left feeling disconnected and daunted by not belonging again. Knowing that I fit in very few places, my need to belong is strong. My need to belong without compromise is finally growing stronger. Belonging to a place through false impressions isn't actually belonging. It's hiding. I don't need to hide! I have done this my whole life and I am exhausted from hiding. This is my time to shine. A star never feels ashamed or embarrassed by her brilliance. She boldly shines and leads ships through dark waters time and time again. She has shone her brightest her whole life. As would I, if I didn't believe I wasn't meant to. If I didn't believe I wasn't worthy of it. We all shine. We really do. The only facade is the thin layer of false beliefs between you and your luster. Life is an excellent polisher, a master. There is no point in resisting what is inevitably for my own good. I tried, believe me I tried. And I fell flat on my face every, single, time. As I was meant to. If I stayed down on the floor after battling resistance I wouldn't be polished. Being polished is my destiny. I have no idea how shiny I am, yet. But, I am willing to keep showing up to the process to find out.

The women in my circle not only apologized, they rose up. They each met a new higher level of themselves. By my courage to speak up, it showed them that their behaviors are known. That they are affecting another person. They each shared a way that my courage is appreciated by them. K said that my "upfront, outspoken-ness is a source of trust for her." She knows that every time she can count on me to speak what is true for me, and that builds trust. "I am a breath of gold in our circle."

J said I, "am a force, a mighty force of consciousness." That each time we gather she is blown away by my level of self-awareness and courage." Afterward, they held me for a while. Everyone got into a cuddle puddle and I cried and cried and cried. I shed tears of shame, smallness, and non-worth. Letting go of these old beliefs that it's not ok for me to stand in my power. That it's not ok for me to support my inner child. My IC (inner child) was certain that I made many mistakes by speaking up last night and making it harder on the other women. I kept holding my IC and speaking to her. Letting her know that I trust this, I trust them. I trust that we are helping our entire circle to grow. That we are being a beacon!

A said, "You are our teacher, you are always showing us how to honor ourselves and be brave."

There is a great reward for speaking from your soul. Letting those that care for you have the chance to be in the intimate gnarl of your most vulnerable center and hold you there. It's an honor, not a place to fear. It all began with the choice to be conscious. I chose well. I chose me.

As my sisters held me, caught my tears, I could feel my Feral Child growing up. She aged right before me. She, too, let go of some of her armoring. She became a young lady and released her Feral-ness! It was profound, something I could never have anticipated or planned. That is the power of being seen, the power of love.

The radical part of my parenting isn't correcting my mistakes, keeping my heart open, or learning how to be a mom. It's listening to the wounded little girl that lives deep, deep inside of me. When I first happened upon her, it was during my shadow work. I called her "Feral Child." She had a companion, "Belonging the Cat." They kept one another company deep in my inner world. They lived together, harmoniously as only two starving things can, without my noticing. I would occasionally feel this deep ache in my heart or a bit of an adult temper tantrum. Yet, I wasn't too concerned about what the cause was.

When I bumped into them, it was a heightened moment of numbed pain. I could no longer ignore this place inside of me. The neglected and abandoned part of myself. I still dance or tiptoe around it. It's the part of my self-love journey that I find to be most problematic. When I think of Feral Child, I see her in our daughter's eyes. Mae has a similar spirit to my inner child. The feral child wants little if nothing at all from me. She recoils at my touch and crouches at the sound of my voice. The only thing she will accept from me is a pure presence. She doesn't trust me or believe that I will stick around for her. I don't blame her, I have proven myself to

157

be unreliable. A real shit. I've let her absorb the brunt of our trauma and left her buried deep within my psyche. We both bellow at the exposure. I think there was an equanimity that both of us tolerated. Now, Belonging the Cat is a lot less tolerant of my antics or abandon. She is very protective of Feral Child and claws at me whenever I edge near Feral. I find a comfort in Belonging's behavior as my best friend was once a cat named Mittens.

Mittens was also protective of me. He stood by me the night the man came into my room and crushed me under the weight of him. Soon after that, Uncle Cole took mittens and he never came back again. When I frantically looked for him, as I ran back and forth through the house, calling his name, Cole smugly stopped me and asked me what I was looking for.

"I am looking for mittens, have you seen him?"

"Yeah, I saw him, as I threw in a dumpster a few hours ago!"

I was devastated. When Faith finally arrived back at the house, I heard her and Cole arguing. She flew out of the house and said she tried to find Mittens but returned empty-handed. Losing Mittens that way was the hardest day. Almost as hard as losing Bobo. Mittens was a gift from my grandmother, and I cherished him. The way he would bap my nose each morning and wake me up for school. He waited for me every day after school and would snuggle under my neck each night. We were one another's friends. I looked to him for comfort and would like to think I gave him comforts as well. It was the two of us in the house of haze.

Belonging and Feral are no doubt ghosts of the trauma I endured. Feral looks gaunt and tattered, just as I felt for many months after the incident. The only thing I could remember was passing out all the time.

It wasn't for lack of food, which was a reality for me growing up with the ketchup on white bread, or grilled government cheese sandwiches. The taste of that cheese was like no other. I am pretty sure it was pure cheddar and was delicious when melted between toast.

I was fainting from fright. Anytime I heard a deep voice or felt the shadow of a larger body around me, I would black out.

On my way to pick up pizza, a man was riding right up the rear of my Toyota Highlander (I call her "The Pearl"). She's a pearlescent beauty that was found amongst the clams at the dealership. She is a strong runner, well maintained, and didn't cost us a fortune.

I could feel the anger boiling up inside of me. This anger wasn't because of him, it's been lying dormant in my heart space for weeks. Each time I get behind the wheel I feel threatened and afraid, uncertain of what the other people on the road are going to do. This has been a theme for months, now that I think about it. We have averted a few bad accidents and strange scenarios that left me uneasy.

Today, after this man, my anger and I grabbed the pizza, feeling the fury beneath my skin. As I began to back out of the lot, the car next to me jumped ahead and pulled out first. That was it. I BLEW! I began talking to myself in the car about why I was so angry. *"I am SO PISSED! Why the hell does this keep happening? Do people think I am invisible?!"*

I will avoid the whole process and get to the heart of this matter. My driving experiences are reminders of when I was a young girl, living in chaos. I often felt invisible, that no one even noticed a living breathing human was there and needed to be assured of her safety. I wasn't assured, soothed, or comforted. I swallowed down my fear and continued moving forward. So many swallows, all leading to this massive build up and explosion. I am sick of being invisible and unseen. Sick of feeling afraid and uncertain if it's ok to be seen in this world. So tired of supporting all the people in my life, while ignoring myself. I need my own security and trust and love and shouldering. I need to know that I matter to myself.

I held my little girl (Feral Child) so tightly and kept rocking her, letting her know I see her. I feel her. I am here for her. Rocking and coddling my inner child who is so afraid. Her letting me near her is a testament of how far we have come. She has lived deep inside; bearing the weight of how often I have swallowed down my fear, tears, or voice—too afraid to let my needs be known for fear of being further rejected. The unearthing of these inner lands is painful, slow and repetitive.

My inner child is asking to be heard and safe. To be felt by me, without any assertion of anything. Only to hold her and let her know she is safe with me. She is. I am. We are. It's a new phase of my growth and self-acceptance. Letting her lead and have time with me in a way that no longer feels threatening is in itself a process. One that I am patiently learning to cultivate within my inner world. Giving her a permanent place that is no longer in threat. A place she can rest safely within me. Without fear of my inner judge, bully, victim, and abuser. A room with a view and door with no lock. A soft place to rest and be.

This is the hardest part of my walk. Learning to sink into the wounds and trust that I can bear the intensity, while sharing this with our family. I came in the from the car, pizza boxes in hand and tears flooding my face. Mae and Alex greeted me with open arms.

"What's wrong, Mom?" She asked.

"Honey I opened up a painful place tonight." As I shared the story, they both wrapped me in their arms and listened. They held me. Their mom. Our children are being shown that it's ok to hurt. That one can live from feeling the depths their soul aches, and it's not permanent. We huddled, and I cried. It lasted for maybe ten minutes. Then life went on as usual.

This is the emboldened part of mothering, letting them see the real side of me. I, too, can crack and let the tears out, that life hurts me and isn't perfect. I am filled with battle scars that occasionally open up and need air to heal. This is where the trust comes in, trusting that it's healing me and helping my inner world to become whole, slowly reducing the expanse in my vista. I deserve this level of attention to self, and my wounded Feral Child. She has endured much for our continued evolution. It feels good to slow down, listen and reward her courage. I see you my dear. You are home.

I never knew how Faith felt, if anything she was doing in her life was scary, or troubling for her. She never spoke of herself in a human or womanly way. I guess this was her way of keeping me protected from the difficulties she was facing. For me, I already knew things were difficult. I was being affected by the world around me, and I wasn't to speak of our realities. My form of communication was through acting out. It was my way of letting my inner storms free in the world, without the use of words. My words didn't seem to matter to her, or the few people I interacted with throughout the day.

In my younger years, I felt sad and alone a lot. Once around a group of kids, I didn't want to push them away be being the complainer, or whiner. I tried my best to match their energy, opinions, and mannerisms. Taking what they put out and recycling it as my own. It was another way for me to blend and be accepted. I hadn't developed a sense of self, or autonomy. I was a clinger and hung on tight to anyone who would let me.

Sometimes I worry that I share too much with our children and that this isn't healthy. How can one's truth not be healthy? I tell them when I am tired, scared, worried, or unsure. I tell them what it takes for me to be here taking care of the daily duties. I also tell them when I think it sucks. I don't make it about them. I feel as a whole, society asks too much of one person, let alone the entire Earth. Our earth mother must be fatigued from all that she gives and absorbs each day. I know that as an empathic mother in my own home I feel this way. There is little time for the things that truly matter; play, nature, quiet, stillness, connection, conversation. In one given day we may only see each other for three hours and some of that time is while driving to an activity. My entire presence is not with our children. I struggle with the constant state of distractions and duties that once made me feel that I mattered. I took on running the house and being a dutiful homemaker as an assurance to me being important and being necessary.

I no longer need this layer of security and we are in our routines so deeply that it takes three times the amount of energy to unbury myself. These are the things I wished my mother spoke of. To show me what really mattered when walking the Earth. Doing laundry, making meals, shopping, running errands—none of it matters when the clock stops. These are supposed essentials, and the only thing that is essentially important to me is knowing who a person is. Knowing what keeps them awake at night, what they dream of, why sets them alive, how it feels to be in a relationship with them. By the time I finish with the so-called essentials, I am too tired to engage or be attentive to what fills my own heart and soul.

These are the conversations we are having in our home. How do we manage the load as a unit, to leave space for knowing who we are as individuals?

Walking along a trail today, I took notice of an Ivy vine, quietly climbing up the tree, gently making its way to the sun. The image is symbolic of my journey. The majority of my life I have been a vine: needy, clingy, grasping. I elevated my position in life with the support of other people, often seeking validation, and having my okay-ness in the world come from someone else telling me so. I felt anxious and uncertain if I could do something well, without another's approval each step along the way.

I admit that I was codependent. The thing is, how was I to know this? I didn't have perspective, until one day I did. I caught myself sucking the life from others, exhausting those around me, because my needs were great. I desperately wanted for them to meet all of my needs, and "make" me happy. If they couldn't, I would pit one person against another. The one who wasn't making me happy, now the bad guy. The one who would make me happy (always, only temporarily) the good guy. It's embarrassing and saddening for me to see these patterns of behavior, yet, scary if I never did! The only way to begin changing dysfunction is to admit it exists.

As I continue along my path, I'm finding my way and growing my own roots, being with others without demand, no longer harboring an expectation of a certain outcome. I can be present, connected, then move about without holding on.

I take care of my needs, desires, and wants, without making my happiness someone else's responsibility. It's a joy to see this transition and growth within myself. I celebrate this moment, this awareness. Also, every situation, person, experience that has helped me to plant my own roots! It's the greatest offering of trust and love one can give.

What was once co-dependence in my relationships was really a refusal to depend on me. It took much practice to learn that putting yourself first in thought and care was important. The issue with putting my needs and care first, is that I am very vulnerable. It leaves me exposed to the potential of someone saying no or rejecting me. Most frightening is to be thought of as selfish. The more painful realization is how often I reject myself and my own needs because of the potential fear of someone else's rejection. The person I am most afraid of being intimate with is me.

"No" is one of my favorite words. Every time I say no to something that doesn't feel right, I am leaving room to say yes to something that does. Or do I? During my shower is where I do my very best thinking. I was looking over my past week, reviewing how it went for me and preparing myself to make adjustments for the week to come. What I noticed were many ways I tell myself "NO." Now, at first glance this might now seem so bad. "What's the big deal with setting personal boundaries?" Absolutely nothing, except this isn't a boundary, it's me protecting myself. And then the question, "How many times a day do I tell myself no?"

Here's what I captured over a few days' time.....

No to exercise
No to going to bed earlier
No to reading my book
No to listening to music while I cook
No to cooking all the greens
No to writing my book
No to listening to praise from my husband
No to calling my aging family members
No to finishing the laundry
No to beginning my podcast
No to writing out business proposals
No to walking my dog
No to drinking more water
No to letting people know who I am 100%

No to letting go of my fears
No to speaking my truth 100%
No to meditating

So on and so on. So many no's to things that is in fact EXCELLENT for my wellbeing. What am I saying yes to? Distractions. Putting non-essentials first, I am afraid of being my strongest, most powerful self. So I hide. I tell myself no, not today. The essentials to your brilliance can wait another day. You're not ready to be out in the world. Just keep doing the things that are mediocre and you'll be ok. Except I'm not ok. I am angry, frustrated and mad at myself for listening and battling this inner voice of fear, doubt, and self-sabotage.

My soul is the one encouraging me to exercise, write this book, meditate, keep strong connections with the elders of our family, and be receptive to the kindness and love of others. My ego can't take me being good to myself because it's far more accustomed to having the say in my life. It is comfortable in suffering. Smoldering. Stifling my growth.

Ego feels safest when I am not taking any steps toward my personal power. Now that I have witnessed my own inner struggle, calling it out and into the light, I am going to challenge myself to say NO to my fears and Ego.

No, to letting myself be persuaded to stay small and insignificant to myself.   This work isn't easy, and it's the only way to wholeness. Seeing my own inner games and BS, calling myself out, publicly, and getting to work. I have much to share in the world and it won't be known if I keep telling myself, NO.

Here's to YES! Yes to me, because I matter.

Imagine that the shield around one's heart is really made of transparent paper similar to rice paper. The heaviness and strength of that armor comes from perception and not reality. The armor seems strong and powerful, when in fact it's light, effortless, and can be broken with one breath.

Chapter Eight
Divorcing vs. Divorce

No one can measure or judge the depths of one's heart, or, better yet, their needs. Adam and I made many choices from a place of hurt, more specifically of denial.

Sarah was busying herself in the kitchen putting the finishing touches on her mung bean soup. If you ever meet Sarah and she offers you a cup of her soup, do yourself the merit of saying yes. I personally do not like mung beans, they make me blow up like a balloon—a very happy and contented balloon—nevertheless, I'm pretty sure it says it on the packaging as a warning; "Too many mung beans will cause you to grow in size and possibly float." That's the thing about Sarah's soup; I forget about all of the side effects and savor each sublime bite.

"I've figured it out," I said.

"Figured what out?" she asked.

"What Adam and I are doing with our... whatever you would call our marriage at this point. We are going through a divorcing."

"Ooooh," she said, "tell me more."

"We are verbing our way through what would otherwise be a final decision." She gave a grunted chuckle.

"I mean if you think about, don't most marriages go through a divorcing? Before the finality of a divorce?"

"Hmmm, I want you to keep expanding on this thought," she said, "as I am always curious if C. and I would have had a different outcome if we were having these types of conversations with other people, prior to our divorce."

"Right, exactly! I think it's so important to understand the process, and what is taking place, before making a forever decision! Talking through the difficulties, confusion, and uncertainty with other people, letting go of the facade that we have a 'good' relationship. I'm tired of living in denial, or pretending in social circles, because no one is talking about their real relationship. It feels softer to say; 'Hi, I'm Brigid, and I'm in a divorcing process. Things aren't great right now, and they're not over.' I wonder if that would invite someone else to stand up and say, hello.

"Adam and I are divorcing our ideals, our promises, our expectations, our beliefs, and our vows. We are actively in the process of deconstructing everything we used to rely on to keep us together as a couple. We are in motion. The time to decide our fate is not now. We are still moving in the mess, trying to sort things out and figure out who we are here. Can you imagine if people took the time to divorce the illusion by which the relationship once stood, to rebuild with tools of what has the hope to hold and grow where they are heading? I think the original structure we relied on in our relationship wasn't stable enough to carry us to the end. As we've grown as individuals, we have stretched the perimeters of our marital homestead. We are in a divorcing."

Anger and Grudges

We have experienced many twists in our long road of relating to one another. It wasn't hard in the beginning. I never saw a fault with Adam. I was too busy trying to prove my worth to him, to make note of anything being awry. I can say there were warning signs, little things I noticed with how he interacted with his peer group, his parents, his siblings. I tucked them away in my memory bank. None of it seemed pressing at the time, but these little pockets of memory would pop up when I needed them to.

We used to spend most of our time and money having fun. We would go to the theatre, travel, shop, have fancy dinners, party, and save. We literally didn't have a worry for ourselves, everything was running smoothly. He was helping me deal with leaving home, and still helping Faith financially. I was learning how to be a partner, and roommate. The pressures were new and minimal. We were still in the honeymoon phase of our relationship. Adam had angst and wanted to break away from society. I was still neck deep in the confines of societal structures, norms, and expectations. Still pondering what it meant to be a productive member of society, a good person. I wanted to have a great job, climb the ladder of success, and go back to school. Seeing that I never invested in my education during my earlier years, there was still time to become something, a somebody.

For now, I was content being a somebody to him. I was beginning to meld in with his peer group and deepen our relationship. When troubles would arise, they were seemingly simple arguments; about which direction the toilet paper roll was facing, or how I liked to stack the dishes. It all seemed so innocent and benign. Little did either of us know that the foundation for how we communicated mattered more than we, or I, gave attention to. I always liked to brush it aside and make him happy. I just wanted him to be happy with me, with us, with my funny ways of doing things. Initially, I thought these slight annoyances were typical. As the years moved along, we began to argue in front of friends and family. Now this behavior opened a door for others' opinions of our relationship. Most often people sided with me. They thought Adam was petty and nit picking me. More than once I heard the words; "You're in a verbally abusive relationship." Those words stung, but never stuck. How could I be in an abusive relationship? Faith was in an abusive relationship; Adam is nothing like my step-dad. I am hard to live with and have my many flaws. At the time I didn't show my dark side. I kept it well hidden and manipulated situations to be seen as the good guy. Through our time together, this strategy has caused many arguments between Adam and me. He feels unseen and heard, victimized by my behaviors. He is the one who feels abused! I was still in denial of any of the "labels" put on our relationship.

We traveled across the country together before getting married. This proved to be a good idea, because when we arrived back in Ohio, we hated one another. I couldn't wait to get out of the car and never see him again. Until two days later when I missed him terribly. I was mourning the death of our relationship, as well as any prospects of us being a couple again. It was miserable.

Being back home with Faith was another humbling experience, though she did manage it well. She was excited to have me back and stationary in Cleveland. I brought her comfort, just as Adam once did for me.

Over time Adam and I began talking with one another and made a go at it again. This time we were certain we'd learned from our mistakes. We were only apart for a few months, most of which I spent hustling to get a job, car, and stability, while managing my dysfunctional relationship with Faith. The struggle was living in her one room apartment, sleeping on her lumpy couch. It had a hideous rose pattern on it and was tinged with a constant smell of stale cigarettes. She had slowed down in her later years and was no longer drinking (I still suspected she was doing some type of pills). She was aging and devoting more of her time to being in service to the Republican Party. She would volunteer at the voting polls every election and assist various local candidates with campaign drives.

The scene we were living was reminiscent of our earlier years on W. 117th; little money, prospects, and trying to pretend everything was normal. I was talking with a few different friends about renting an apartment together, trying to find any way that I could to get farther away from her, the memories I didn't want to face.

Adam and I decided to take some of our money we had mutually saved and buy land. This way we could begin building an off the grid life on our own property, without the need to travel and hustle. After viewing several parcels in western New York, we settled on our eight acres, which sits nestled atop a hill, completely wooded, surrounded with a rich flora. It was a big decision for us as we weren't married, still unsure if we would make it in a long-term relationship. This was another straw we grasped at to keep our relationship and dreams alive.

We moved into a small apartment in Jamestown, New York. We went to our land each day to trim trees, blaze trails, and prep it for plantings. Each day was difficult because we have very different ideas of how we wanted to manage our land, of where things were going to be planted, of our styles—and, once again, our communication was ineffective. After a few months of being on the land we had another blow out fight and I went home for good.

As we both went about our ways, finding a new way of reintegrating in our lives in Cleveland, I began yearning to be with him again. Each day was hard to manage without Adam. I no longer had a sense of wellness without his presence. The irony—I didn't have a sense of wellness with his presence either. All the mixed-up feelings drove my longing stronger and harder than ever. I would feel an extreme sense of loneliness and failure. I had many chances with him. We just couldn't make it work. His romance, care, and generosity were no longer enough to make a relationship work. For once I felt hopeless.

The phone rang around 6:00 A.M. one morning. Faith grabbed it, and handed me the phone. It was the Kent State Police Dept. Adam was involved in a head-on car crash; he and the other driver were both ok and soon to be discharged from the hospital. Adam kept asking for me and gave them my phone number. I was so distraught at the thought of him being killed, that I immediately rushed down there to save him! I no longer cared about our struggles, he needed me, and I had to be there with him. He moved down to Kent to continue his education and get his Master's degree. I kept my job, and moved in with him in Kent; assured that this time we would be ok. We were both given a new lease on life after his accident. Some of the pettiness we had between us, melted away. We were committed to having a happy life together.

Adam proposed to me for a second time, in front of his parents. Unlike the first proposal, this one felt heavy. Our first engagement was romantic and a complete surprise; he had woven strands of our hair together and made a promise ring for me, got down on one knee and vowed to love me for eternity, and asked if I would do him the honor of being his wife. This proposal fell flat, though it was sweet in gesture and attempt. The excitement I once had at being his wife was no longer vibrant in our relationship. I now was feeling needy and dependent on him. After all, I had proven to myself that I needed him. Without him, I was always longing and missing something. Life without Adam had a new hue of grey. I said yes, and we planned our whole ceremony in under five months.

The wedding planning was fun; we communicated well, and were finally a functioning team. I felt that we had gotten back on some sort of track. We were partnering and working for common goals. It was refreshing! After our marriage and honeymoon, we settled in Kent, while he continued working toward his master's. I would commute every day from Kent to Cleveland and back again for my job. Things were running the smoothest they had for us in quite some time. Though now we were poor, no longer living the high life. There was a simple sweetness that I appreciated. I enjoyed our quiet nights at home, or occasionally having visitors. That was another thing I never quite figured out how to handle gracefully. Whenever I knew we were having company, I would get myself all worked up; about the cleanliness of our apartment, what types of food we would serve. Always trying to micromanage everything, to perfection. I would literally get myself into a tizzy.

We had this parallelism in our home, where I wanted his help, support, and assurance, but I also pushed him away, rejected and argued with any suggestions he made. I wanted to be supported, while being in control. It was the letting go of control piece I never could quite manage.

When I found out we were expecting I was excited and scared to death, mainly scared because of my own demons. Also, how would having a baby affect our relationship? I didn't feel that we had things nailed down tight in our marriage at the time, and now we were bringing a child into our relationship. Adam constantly assured me everything would be A-Okay!

We were mostly on the same page when it came to the expectations of our delivery, setting up the nursery, what we wanted for our child. Our main goal was to stay as close to the Earth as possible. Have a natural childbirth. We tried to find someone who would help us deliver at home, but there were laws prohibiting home births in our city. I wanted to nurse and to be home with the baby for as long as possible and bond. We agreed we didn't need much more than one another and a comfortable home. We had everything we needed, except, we never accounted for if things went wrong, nor did we take into consideration how stressful it might be. We were the first ones in our close circle to be pregnant. I didn't have a lot of modeling around me, or people to ask questions of.

The delivery was traumatic. Alex got stuck in the canal and with the help of nurses, our midwife, and the doctor; they miraculously popped my pelvis to free him. Leading up to the delivery, I wasn't dilating naturally and they induced labor. All of these unexpected circumstances increased our stress level, and inability to communicate well. It was hard to make sound decisions in haste, and stressed, while also wrestling with the disappointment of not having a perfect delivery. I laugh at the thought of this now, three kids later, but at the time, it never occurred to me that things could go wrong. When they went wrong, I blamed him.

It's sad to admit that the birth of our children did cause some of my biggest grudges towards Adam. These were the first times in my heart I felt hate towards him. These were our once in a lifetime moments, full of promise and expectation. I was extremely tender, raw and vulnerable during the pregnancies and deliveries of each of our children. I most likely had undiagnosed PTSD from Alex's birth, followed by the trauma of Mae's pregnancy and delivery, and finally my near-death experience with Michael. Each of our children came in with a bang, coupled with intermittent postpartum depression. The fallout was stored in my body. I wanted someone to blame, someone to carry the load of all these traumas. Adam wasn't affected in the same way I was, and I also felt he had a hard time relating to me. Very little in his world changed, he could come and go as he pleased, sleep all night, eat foods he liked, have beer if he wanted. Everything in my world was dedicated to growing, supporting, and nurturing life. I gave up everything familiar in the ways I ate, slept, relaxed, bathed, and related to the outside world.

I enabled Adam by doing everything with the children; all activities, doctors' appointments, outings. I used to ask if he would like to join us and after several years of being disappointed by his unavailability (working all of the time to help us pay on our bills, which never felt as loving as being with us would have), which I took personally, I stopped asking. Which led to more distance and resentments between us, I developed excessive anxiety when it comes to doctor appointments. Ever since Mae's early diagnosis, I have been the one receiving bad news alone at the appointments. I walked in with dread as my co-pilot month after month, year after year. I never noticed dread was there until once I turned to the side and was slapped awake. I lost all composure during a routine doctor visit. The kids were bickering, my stress level through the roof, and our pediatrician who has known me since Alex was a baby, asked if everything was ok. All of the feelings I had tamped down came rushing out; "I am sick of being alone, doing alone, and carrying everything alone, while I am married. I have fatigue on top of fatigue, loneliness, and sadness from raising our children seemingly alone." All of my truths laid out on the floor of our pediatrician's office. She sat with me and let me cry.

Adam devoted himself to working a job that would support our family's needs, while I stayed home to raise our children. Though I didn't know it at the time, I took everything on, to show my worth of being the stay at home mother. I enabled the distance, and disconnect from daily doings with child rearing, to prove I was enough, that I was earning my keep as the parent who stayed home.

He was sympathetic, but not empathetic, so it always felt saccharine sweet to me. I didn't feel like the most important person in his life, or highly valued. I felt more of a commodity.

These are big feelings and grudges to carry in some of the most memorable seasons of our lives together. I didn't articulate myself well. I didn't say, "I really need you. I need to know that I matter to you. I need to know that you care and are concerned for my wellbeing." Instead I closed up and shut down. I lived each day with a painted smile, while slowly withering inside.

Time has a way of leaping when in the newness of building a family. Change of jobs, location, and intense focus on keeping tiny humans alive. My needs, nor his, seemed especially important. Thinking about things like self-care, date night, regular conversations, weren't as important as how many diapers I changed that day, or how often I was feeding the babies. I had just finished nursing Alex when Mae came, had my boobs back for two years, and then gave them to Michael. Knowing me—as a woman, wife, and friend—was all secondary to being a mother.

I was skating on the surface of survival at this time. I told myself that the most important thing was making sure our children were happy. What does that even mean? They are absorbing the energy all around them every day. If I made not fighting with Adam my priority, or keeping my mental wellness in check, or taking time away for me, things most likely wouldn't have fallen apart. We have spent years hanging onto one another by a very thin seam of commitment. When the love felt cold, the conversations ceased eye contact remiss— we hung on with commitment. Our commitment that no matter how bad things were between us, they were never as bad as being without one another, so began the cycle of existing on life support.

"Love without consciousness becomes need, dependency, and control in the name of love."--Dr. Shefali Tsabary

---

I had a sinking feeling about this trip, though it mattered a lot to Adam. I kept resisting everything about it. He was taking our eldest, Alex, across the country on a trip to welcome Alex's rite of passage into manhood. It wasn't the intent that didn't feel right; it was the timeline, and the means of how they would get there. They were driving a thousand miles or more, Adam the sole driver. I finally conceded that maybe I was having irrational fears, and just allow this to be what it was, a father wanting to bond and celebrate his eldest son.

While they were gone, things around the house were quiet and calm. We heard from them occasionally, either via text or a late-night check in. It seemed they were having a great time, but I kept hearing something in Adam's voice that alerted me he wasn't 100% well. I felt relieved hearing from them, yet concerned, because no amount of questioning brought up what was really going on. Upon their arrival, the nagging feelings were confirmed. Adam got out of the car and had a green tinge to his complexion.

"How are you feeling? You don't look well," I said.

"I'm not feeling my best, but I think it's because we pushed to get home and I haven't slept very much."

"Do you think sleep will help your color return, or should we go to the E.R.?"

"Brigid, stop worrying about me, I will be fine."

Those infamous words--similar to his statement "I wish you would worry more about your personality then your weight." *Careful what we speak and wish for!* The usual way I am received by him. I am a worry-wort and don't really have any basis for all of my questions and nagging. Even though I am an empathic intuitive!

Adam ended up, that evening, being rushed by me to the Emergency Room, where they found two pulmonary embolisms. This news was scary and uncertain. We were waiting to see which way they would go. They dislodged from his leg and headed straight for his heart, once through the heart they would either go to his head or lungs. Neither of these options felt good to know, worse to wait for.

The look on his face was still suggesting I shouldn't worry. As I sat there, looking at his reassurance, I wanted to scream; "Aren't you afraid, too? Why am I the only one admitting this is scary?"

Our children went to his Mother's house, while I stayed with him in the hospital. They were working on him non-stop with fluids, blood thinners, and pain killers. The moment came when the clots moved and he was gasping for air. I knew they went into his lungs. The nurses were giving him high doses of morphine to help him with the pain, which also slowed his breathing, which also helped with the pain. I was watching Adam's life hang in the balance. I had no words. No thoughts other than *Holy shit. How am I going to leave here without him? He can't die, not now, not like this. Our children need their father, I need him.* I prayed. I begged. I prayed. I pleaded. I had to keep removing myself from the room and take a few breaths; to keep myself grounded enough to manage the immense amount of fear that was flooding me.

I was right back to our early years when we broke up and didn't know if we would ever get back to being in relationship with one another. The possible finality of our circumstance was crushing.

After almost 24 hours of being monitored and assisted, they were happy to report the clots had passed and he was out of the woods. Somehow that news didn't feel better. I couldn't believe that he was in the clear. My brain was still in disaster mode.

He was taken into ICU and remained there for several days, as they were keeping him stable, while also running more tests to see if there was any underlying issue that would have caused the clotting. They discovered he has a blood disorder that creates clots. The disorder, coupled with long periods of sitting, was the perfect storm for the blood clots to develop.

Adam finally admitted, "I knew something wasn't right on our way back home. My left leg hurt me and had a pressure in it that I hadn't ever experienced."

While I was thankful he made it home and didn't have this happen en route, I had a sense of dread hanging over me. It felt like another ball was going to drop at any minute. I was in some state of denial or shock, trying to keep myself safe from the potential threat of Adam dying.

As the weeks wore on during his recovery, we did face another issue. They prescribed him Oxycodone to help manage his pain. His chest hurt him for a long time after the clots passed. The pain pills helped to manage his pain, except no one ever told him how addictive the pills are. He tried going off of them cold turkey and became very ill. He looked like a zombie! I couldn't believe that after all he had faced, he was now dealing with withdrawal from prescribed medications. It was awful watching him wean his body off of those pills; sweating, nausea, mood swings, disoriented, fatigue, thirst, shakes. He was in full detox, and there wasn't much to assist him, but time, and nurturing.

My shock wore off, and I was now facing full anger. I was so angry with him for taking the trip, taking the pills, almost dying. Moving through all of the emotions that come with trauma, working through the layers and seeing how much toxicity there was in our relationship. I don't know who I am without him, or how I will manage without him. My dependency on Adam was immense, and something I could no longer allow. At first I dismissed these thoughts, for fear I was pushing him away to prevent myself from being hurt again. The farther away we got from the incident, I realized that all of this was a blessing to both of us. We needed to begin managing our own needs without the expectation of the other.

We were now in the invitation of beginning our divorcing process. Seeing how unhealthy our relationship was for me, I began to unravel our agreements, taking more time for my own passions, desires, and needs to be met outside of our relationship. I began to develop a relationship with the woman who lived inside of me. I didn't know anything about her likes, dislikes, needs, or interests. I had spent the last 15 years worrying about being pleasing and sufficient to another. His near death was a chance for my revival.

Adam invited me to meet him for happy hour at a place near his work. Being unfamiliar with the area, I suggest I swing by his office and pick him up, to alleviate me getting lost. The invitation to meet up was an attempt to keep our relationship alive. As we were eating and idling chatting, I began sharing with him excitedly ways I was envisioning growing my Reiki business. I asked him if he would be willing to share one of my brochures at his work, to see if there was any interest in offering my services to the employees. He flat out declined and said he wasn't comfortable soliciting anything to his employer, and he didn't really believe in Reiki. Everything slowed; I was stunned and felt the heft of disappoint getting ready to wash down my face in tears.

"How can you say this to me? It's like you don't believe in me at all!"

"Maybe I don't."

All the words that were floating in my head stopped and did an *Oh no he didn't.* gesture.

I stared him straight in the eyes, and said, "Thank you for dinner, and your honesty. I will be in the car if you'd like a ride back to yours." I collected my coat and purse, and walked out.

Let's pause here. This was far greater than his statement. This was about me standing up for my dreams, my beliefs, my honor. I knew that asking for his help was a stretch because he does have certain criteria for how he conducts himself at work. For as long as I can remember, he doesn't participate in school or sports fundraisers at work for our children. So, it wasn't a huge surprise that he declined my offer. What jabbed me in the back was his disbelief in my passion. I'd been a Reiki practitioner for over two years, and this was the first time I heard him dismiss my profession.

His non-believing in me was in fact a great gift, because in that moment I realized I no longer had the intentions of proving to him who I was, I was now focused on proving it to myself!

Codependent Martyrdom

Adam has been instrumental in my growth and healing. I believe that over time it has come at a great cost to his own spirit, esteem, and wellbeing. He has given me everything he knows how, which is at times devastating that I am discontent. Few of my own stirrings are because of him. This has taken me several years to unravel. I blamed him for everything that wasn't working in my life. I have been abusive, dismissive, controlling, aggressive, argumentative, and downright awful. Faith used to bear the brunt of my anger. When Adam and I moved in with one another he replaced her as my whipping post. None of these truths are easy to share with the world. Yet, if I do not speak of where we were, you will not fully grasp how much had to change to be where we are.

In our early relationship, Adam was free-spirited and of the world. He believed in the power of the Moon cycles, of living off the earth and breaking free from societal constructs, expectations, and delusions. I was so deeply attached to all of it. I wanted the nice house, cars, vacations, and most importantly to be away from Faith. I missed out on the college experience, as she and I were barely scraping by on our meager incomes. I was still sorting out how to have a career with a limited background, minimal education, and most importantly waning desire. I didn't mind working, but it wasn't my passion. I was still looking for the thing that set my soul on fire. Adam was one of the things that lit me up. His fire was burning hot and he was impassioned. He knew exactly what he wanted. He didn't know how to execute his vision, but he had vision. In my peer group at the time, that wasn't something we spoke of. We mostly all hung out doing what everyone else was doing; going to bars, drinking, or seeing bands, working a dead-end job. Every once in a while, a small group of us would go out on the town and try something new, or we would go away for a weekend. Life was anticipatory with little fuel or sparks of excitement.

I knew that Adam would be good for me. I never asked myself if I was good for him, if I could live the life he was desiring. If I would be willing to contribute to our overall happiness. I can admit that I was taking from him, more than I was giving. We both were hungry to be loved. To matter. And, that we did. Nothing had more of my attention than Adam. He took me on crazy afternoon adventures that would result in blood. I kid you not. We were at a lighthouse in Huron, Ohio, one afternoon. We went on a leisurely walk, which ended in multiple deep cuts, that resulted in scars that I still carry today. He thought it would be fun to walk on the large rocks that lined the break wall. It began just fine, until the rocks were no longer flat, but instead sticking up and juxtapositioned everywhere. I kept falling, my legs shook, face covered in sweat and tears. He kept picking me up, patiently instructing me where to place my foot. We got to the point where it was equal distance to turn around or keep going. My adrenaline was pumping, legs trembling. I had to rely on him to ensure my safety. I trusted him. This is something that was new to me. I trusted very few people, especially men. Later that night, on the boardwalk, he laid a blanket down and serenaded me with his acoustic guitar, Little Wing by Jimi Hendrix. Unforgettable day, moment, love.

Why Adam put all of his eggs into my basket I will never fully understand. I wasn't ready for marriage. I wasn't ready to be loved. I could barely receive his attention, let alone his affections, his heart, or his fears. I was running away from everything that scared me. I wanted to be safe. Having connection and a deeply loving relationship with him was terrifying to me. I felt each day I had to prove I was worthy of him.

It's taken me a long time to stand here in this space of honoring what a complete mess I've made of most everything we have together. I simply couldn't accept that I am worthy to receive this life. That I have a husband who sees all of my darkness, my shame, guilt, despicableness and still chooses me. That I have a man who was been screamed at, threatened, financially burdened, denied sex, and choked. Yes, I tried to choke him. Once. It was more of a feigned attempt in desperation, but, I still did it and it broke trust and safety between us.

He wakes each morning ready to try again. He has so much faith in our relationship. When I first caught a glimpse of his unwavering faith in me broke my heart. I fell into all of my shame and wallowed. *Why does he love me? Why does he trust me? Why does he keep choosing me? I just don't deserve him.* I never fully committed to our relationship, always having the option to run in my back pocket. I pushed hard testing our relationship.

I threw my rings at him more times than I can count. Until one day my engagement ring, the one he had made for me, went missing. I spent two years in mourning over the loss of my ring. *More shame.* It's true when they say that you only miss what you don't have. I missed all the years I spent hating myself and making it Adam's problem. Everything I kept seeing in him, blaming him for, was my own to take back. I projected my self-loathing all over him. I was blind, and I didn't know it. I truly thought I had made a mistake. I chose the wrong man. I thought I deserved someone who would give me more. Let's pause right here. What more could anyone give me? Adam was worn to the quick. He had given everything. Everything. I was blind. He has given me twenty years of his life. That is almost half of my total existence. That's a lot of minutes, hours, days, weeks of getting to know someone. There wasn't anything about me that I was hiding from Adam, I hid from myself. It was easier to accuse him for my unhappiness.

Is one more diaper change going to be the caveat of any relationship? Does it even matter? I thought so. I thought he was a no good rotten father who ignored his children. So I took matters into my own hands. I pushed him farther away, and became the single, married mother. We didn't need him. What good was he anyways? I spent night after night crying myself to sleep, at war with myself, but, with the misguided belief it was his entire fault!

It didn't come as a surprise to our children, or Adam, when I asked for a divorce. We sat in silence in our backyard, watching the purple leaves of our plum tree sway in the breeze, the tree he and his mother planted for Nana on Mother's Day nearly 25 years ago. We had watched that tree fight for her life. She had an infection or infestation of hornets. We kept an eye on her, and tried to assist with cutting the infected area, fertilizing her deep roots. Then we waited. She knew exactly what to do to rejuvenate herself. We needed her wisdom, as we were stuck. We both wanted to keep trying. To keep believing we could make this work. My asking for a divorce was a declaration of my own internal surrender. I finally conceded that I couldn't do "marriage", couldn't fight myself, blame him, and fight both of us, any longer. I simply needed a break. I was fatigued from all of it.

Life: 1, Brigid: 0.

Just as my heart broke outward the day I felt his faith in me, his heart broke inward. It was the final blow. Though I've threatened in the past, we both heard the resolve in my voice that day. We knew that I was serious. His eyes were full of tears that were too stubborn to fall.

Adam looked around the backyard and noted special memories and dreams we had planted in our gardens; he was recalling that we were working towards life goals in the simplest of ways. One plant at a time, each one would yield fruits for years to come. Fruits that would nourish all of our bodies and beautify our gardens.

I no longer felt attached to the gardens, our house, or Adam. Everywhere I looked I felt the neglect and distance that had grown between us. Where once I saw beauty, now I only see abandon. Was this my fate? To abandon the man who devoted his life to me? Is being in a marriage so frightening to me that running is my only option? Where had my dedication gone?

During this time we still shared our home. Our children knew that things were grave. To say our home collapsed would be an understatement. It was cold, bleak and lifeless day after day. We were all suspended in a state of limbo. I put on my best public face each day, with lots of assurances that everything was "ok." We were far away from ok, and I didn't know how to support anyone, including myself. Our children began having intense anxiety as they were just as uncertain as we were. Neither of us had a plan, or the courage to make a swift decision. The desire for divorce hung like a noose around our necks.

I was filled with conflict, shame and remorse. *After all of the personal work I have done, why can I not see a way to make our marriage work? Better still, why aren't*

I happy within in the marriage? I knew that most of what I was experiencing was my distortions being mirrored back to me. I felt trapped between two worlds. I could see my foggy distortions, and I could also see how much . wanted to hide. I didn't want to be responsible for my part in our relationship. After all the hurt I had created in our relationship, would an "I am sorry" really matter? I said it. I said it daily. I also, pretended that he was saying it to me. One of the differences between Adam and I is that he only sees my faults. I am the one who is always doing wrong within our relationship. I would agree that I contribute, and sometimes am the only one. There are still times when the burden has been placed by both of our actions.

Where was I supposed to go when I didn't want to be responsible and I couldn't bring myself to leave? I kept asking for help from the unseen world. I know that my grandmother, father, and mother are all above me listening. I kept trudging along in my stubborn fashion, just assuming that at some point something would have to give way.

I didn't know that something would be our daughter. Mae had cracked under the pressure of our indecision. All of the years he and I have fought, either from being certain I was right, or vice versa. The pressure of parenting with small witnesses to our dysfunction was so humiliating. I thought for sure we would have figured out how to be a strong couple by the time our children came. When that didn't happen, I had hope in us really getting our act together before they could talk. Nope, still not there. Ok, maybe by the time they are in school, we will have this on lock down. Nope, getting colder. Now they are teenagers, with their own impressions of what love should be, how it looks, what is right, what is wrong. AND, they are giving us their opinions of our how screwed up we are about all of it. YIKES.

Listening to her in therapy was eye opening. The pressure she is under every day, with wondering if her own heart will stop, if we will divorce, if she will ever be liked by the "normal" people. When will life get easier? She said she didn't ask to be born; we "chose that for her!" Shit, wait, what? My guts ripped out and were thrown about on the floor. *What do you mean we chose to have you? We fought for you! We did all of the what-if scenarios and the odds were in your favor. We never would have proceeded if your life would be compromised.* And there it was. The same thing I did with Mae I am doing with Adam. I am fighting. Fighting to prove I wasn't a bad wife. Fighting to prove all those naysayers before we married. Fighting to show the world that we make good decisions. Fighting to approve of my own choices. She was right. She never asked to be born differently. I never asked to be loved, unconditionally. Sometimes we get exactly what we need, not what we want.

I didn't know how to live my life without drama, probably since I was a little girl, and definitely since I can remember, my life has been filled with drama. Either self-induced or by association. Clueless--that life could be lived without constant flux and chaos. I have been living in a play; changing characters, roles, sets, and scenes. All the while not being aware that what I really was searching for, seeking and in desperate need of was my truth. What the hell did I really want? What would I be willing to do? What could I count on in my life? Most importantly, what could I give?

The audience of this play was paying too high of a price. It was time to become acquainted with myself in a way I wouldn't have believed I was ready for. Leaving Adam was easy. Staying to sift through the rubble -- now that is something I haven't tried, in my whole life! I always have my running shoes with me. They are a safety net for when life becomes too difficult. I can always cut and run. I watched Faith do it my whole life, it seemed usual. Doesn't everyone leave when they've had enough? I didn't realize that in life you can make a mountain of mistakes and still have the chance to make them whole again. With our marriage crumbling and our daughter flailing, there weren't a lot of options.

It was time to take responsibility for myself.

What can I offer here?

What can I do?

Where am I making things harder?

One of the differences between Adam and me is our spiritual life. Where once I was forced to believe in God and obey his rules, I shied away from the Catholic Church, and my intuition, for many years. But when things became really hard in my life, I did leave a little window inside of my heart for God, The Creator, and the Universe—something bigger than myself to listen to. I needed a friend that would listen to all of my fears and remind me that I am going to be ok. When I was spinning from Faith dying, Mae healing, and not saving any time for myself, I needed to know that it wouldn't always be this way. When my panic attacks began, and I was afraid to leave my house, I needed someone other than my inner circle, to begin showing me a way. Any way that would help alleviate the fears. I prayed. I begged. I prayed more. Little by little, I began receiving glimpses of my prayers being answered. I began noticing subtle ways that this unseen force was responding to my prayers.

Needing to take responsibility for myself and my participation in our marriage, my prayer was answered when one day I saw a post on Facebook. A woman in a business group that I am a part of (which was another answer from the Universe) was offering 10 weeks of free shadow coaching. Hmmm, I've heard of this shadow work, through Sarah, but I didn't know a lot. I reached out to Linda and expressed an interest in her coaching. She replied with an appointment time for her to interview me, to see if we would be a good fit.

Simultaneously, through journaling and meditation, I was beginning to see the path that I had laid between Adam and me. It began as codependency, and now I had written him out of my story. I came to a chapter in my life story where I no longer needed him. I found him to be a hindrance, rather than an asset. He was making things very hard for me and never wanted to listen or connect with me. He only wanted to condemn. I remember my therapist asking me why I speak of everything in the singular. I would always say me or I. I never said we, us, or together. There came a point in our marriage when we cracked. The fissure grew to the size of a large cavern. By the time I noticed it, it felt too grand to repair. Everything that once held us together would fall into this abyss. There was Adam on one side, me on the other, shouting to be understood across this grand chasm. I no longer can say if it was inevitable—if it was exactly what we needed to begin growing, or if it was carelessness. What I know is it happened to us, between us, and for us.

Our failing marriage, because it's the most important relationship I have made by choice, was the catalyst for my spiritual awakening.

My choice to stay and learn is commitment, unlike anything I have offered to anyone in my life. This devotion is healing not only me, but my lineage. I am healing generations of failed marriages in my ancestry. I come from a line of women who had a "men optional" mentality. That is true, to a point. In my life I need partnership, I need relationships that uplift and elevate my heart, my consciousness, my purpose. If I had run away from Adam when things became unbearable, I would have missed the resurrection, which has been the most beautiful birthing of my life! Yes, this may sound in contrast to having children. The difference is that my body knew how to create life. The re-birth of our love and commitment has come from one hard, treacherous step after the next. Not always carefully placed but done with intent. The intentions are to be more aware, kind and generous than we were yesterday, to keep looking at one another's flaws to understand where we were missing the glory.

Through my shadow coaching I came to learn a lot about mirrors and projections. Most of the things I found intolerable in Adam were actually parts of me that I projected outwardly unto him. Every time I accused him of not listening, being cold, harsh and distant, he was my mirror, helping me to see the ways I was doing this inside of myself. I was ignoring myself. I was cold, harsh and distant to myself. It wasn't that he was trying to hurt me. He was trying to help me see more of myself, for my own healing. This may or may not have been conscious on his part. He was, however, consistent in holding the mirror for me.

Adam helped me go from a survivor mentality to being curious of what a life of thriving would look like. It's something that I am trying to work with every day. I used to stuff our refrigerator and pantry with food; for fear that we wouldn't have enough. Through constant effort and letting go, I've begun to heal that mentality within me, just as I am learning to be respectful with finances and not careless, to not see money in a grasping, clinging way. Faith would blow through any money she had, her mentality was enjoy it while it lasts. Except that in her later years, she had nothing, just as in her earlier years. She was still depending on us to take care of her financial needs. I, too, learned that money was a limited resource to be used up. When I write this, I think it strange seeing the words coupled; "limited resource to be used up." Any resource that is limited should be cherished, savored, and used sparingly. As I continue along the continuum of my life, I am learning that money is a tool. As with all tools, the better cared for, the longer they last, the more that can be built with them and appreciated for latter generations. We still have tools from Adam's grandfather. He knew how to take good care of his tools, as did Nana. The two of them paid for the house we live in in six years; he was a window washer, she a homemaker and part time commercial cleaner. The two of them had respect for their earnings and used it appropriately for needs, not wants.

When Nana was alive I could have fared well to listen more than reject her knowledge. She did try to help me; I was too full of myself to listen.

That's the thing about being in armor; I was always trying to protect my pride. My "right-ness", so full of my own armoring and protective nature that I didn't have any room to listen, to try or to believe that another person could help me, love or support me. I "had" to help myself. It's what I knew, it was my creed.

The Climb

I blew up our lives and as the pieces are coming back down, we are trying to reorganize the way we see our marriage, our coupling, and the lives we are working towards every day. I want to tell you that everything between us is normal (whatever that really means), or, our lives are on track, and that we are more in love than ever. The truth is we are still figuring this out, our commitment has grown, but love isn't an extensive enough of a word here. Love has numerous connotations and perceptions. We are on the frontlines of commitment, digging in, dodging bullets and being purposeful with our actions to make it through another night. Why? Why not just get a divorce? It's not that big of a deal, in fact it's easier than ever, and you no longer are shamed for doing so. Why do we stay?

I can only answer for myself. This is where I find the distinction between a divorcing process: Leaving behind beliefs, vows, traits, and baggage that brought you to a breaking point in the relationship. It's in the break one can decide if they want to forge a new path, be a pioneer in the way they are in partnership with another, or have the finality of a divorce. It's all a matter of choosing what is best and healthiest for you. No one can decide the means by which relationships work. I have seen evidence of most long term (10 years, or longer) marriages going through a divorcing process. A time when the couple reevaluates the terms and agreements they are willing and able to honor with one another.

Now that I can see my part, I see where and how I have acted irresponsibly. I know that I am not the best in relationships, I'm learning. Tomorrow he can decide he no longer chooses me, or I can do the same. For now, this is where I am in my consciousness, my heart, and my honoring. I want to know, if even for one day, what it feels like to be whole, open, and full hearted in relationship. There is always a new way of doing the same thing. I know this in my bones; I am here to show myself it is possible. This isn't a loveless marriage, it's a conscious evolution through the many faces and depths that love can travel, once the fantasy fades, consciousness steps in.

"The qualities keeping this marriage together: I am the bone, you are the ligaments."--Adam Hopkins

---

Perceptions

We have been partnered for almost twenty years. Through all that we have experienced, we both have our variation of the same scenario, a lens by which we are both filtering the experience. My lens isn't pure, clear, or even unbiased. Most of what I have experienced and filtered served some aspect of my personality, my shadow, my inner child, my fearful self, my righteousness, etc. I do not know what it is like to be in a relationship with purity. It is my passion in life to keep exploring past my edges to find the places I hide, deny, or protect. It is what I want my children to see in me as their mother; that life isn't made of perfect people. Happiness isn't something you strive for, it's a state of awareness readily available. Relationships are not always hard or dysfunctional. Everything is a chance to deepen, expand and grow from. I have a limited capacity for joy and happiness. Finding more comfort in my dense, darker self. It has taken m many missteps to find my way back to my light, in order to glean and shine in the world.

Our children have seen the contrast of which I am their whole life, along with my battle with perceptions, fear, and ignorance of my personal strength. I felt shame about my marriage, that we weren't the perfect couple, happy family, living the fairytale. I used to be embarrassed of my struggles, and trappings of the limiting stories--that I am too emotional--too intense--too much, or conversely not enough. I have busted through the shroud of pretending, to expose them to human struggles that I don't feel are singular. Marriages, relationships, inner battles are a part of life's lesson plan. Teaching me how to work through foggy lenses of misperceptions may in fact be my legacy to our family. A legacy that I am proud to experience, and share.

Calling Back Projections

My marriage is not a singular relationship; it is the pinnacle of all of my relationships. They say, "What one gives, one receives." I never believed this old wives tale I used to hear growing up, or, "Do unto others as you would have done unto you." Again, these are outdated, who-do-they-think-they-are, sayings. I have learned firsthand that the state of our disconnect was a result of my lack of giving. I began to pull away, ignore, dismiss, and reject anything that Adam had to offer me. It wasn't in one fell swoop; more subtle, almost unrecognizable.

He would hand me a napkin— "No thank you, I have my own."

Or he would grab the door for me, and I would push past, not even saying thank you.

Or wake up in the middle of the night to take care of one of the babies, and I would snap at him he wasn't doing it right—when in fact he wasn't doing it my way.

I have countless examples of the way I stopped paying attention to his attempts at showing me his love. That he was paying attention, and I hurt him repeatedly by my lack of awareness. I lost touch with how to receive his love. It used to be a given, when it was just the two of us. I was uber vigilant in soaking up his affections and attention. I had in my mind some other way, something that was better, more of a gesture, I don't even know what it would be, but there was a block or belief in my heart that prevented me from no longer noticing the signs of his love. It would appear I was being intentionally obtuse. We argued about the mishaps, never really going beyond the argument to feel where we had broken apart. I can say it was all me, I can say it was him, it means nothing when the pain is beyond bearable. The blame only deepens the pain and divide in the relationship.

We tried therapy that helped for a little while. Our therapist was trying to teach us new ways of communicating. Just as in private, once we hit our edge in a session, we never went back. We also tried following tips and advice from online articles. Both of us cared about the health of our marriage, but, in truth, we always cared more about who was right.

This stubborn, stale place helped me set voyage into my own healing journey that would inevitably help the health of our whole family. Not because I was forcing new ideas, philosophy or my will upon them. Because inside, I was changing, the way I listened was slower, more patient, and kind. The way I spoke changed as well. The way I stood in a room, instead of flying around with my finger pointing outwardly, I looked within.

Everything that has happened between us has helped me to connect with rivers of compassion, empathy and understanding. It is because of the care I have for myself, our children, and our relationship that I am an intrepid explorer of consciousness and growth. Learning how to receive the places in our marriage I denied and didn't want to believe had anything to do with me, brought me to my knees in humility. What I was not able to give as far as commitment and loving acceptance in our marriage, is a direct reflection to level of abandon I have within myself. My refusal to see that I have not yet fully owned and accepted myself exactly as I am.

There comes a moment in the relationship when you may forget what brought you to one another. Like castaways arriving on an abandoned island—while the trees are green, the air is crisp, the sea is blue, and partial surroundings are familiar --you must begin again, as it's not home. You begin with caution, as to not rush to taste or consume anything that may be of harm. Like a child, curious, you wish to rush along to be back to the comforts of home. Where is that place, home?

The only home I know where I belong is in my heart. I trust her, I listen to her, and I know her more intimately than any other person. It's when I guard her that I falter, that I feel lost, scared, trepidations. To lead with my heart is to dance with my soul.

The moment you decide to receive instead of resist, the world rushes to greet you.

Chapter Nine

Dreaming

L iving in a small cottage along the Atlantic Ocean, you learn to pay attention. The air smells a bit tangy before a storm. Salt lands more to the feet when it's high tide. I relished the cool feel that ebbs from our stone walls. The wind howling through the cracks the mortar no longer clung to. Each day, as I walked along the shore listening to the winds, she spoke to me, teaching about resistance, fortitude, and surrender. It was hard to surrender in her graces, she is powerful, and I human. How is a human to stand in the strengths of the wind spirit and not be blown over by her ferocity? Where do you succumb to surrender there?

It was on this particular evening that I remembered that very question. The sea was angry, pulsing and smashing at the shoreline. I huddled in my cot, blanket overhead, paying close attention to the crackling in our fireplace. I could always tell when the fire was low by the sound of the pops and crackles. It wasn't time yet to put another log on the fire, so I stayed buttoned up in my cot.

The wind, she snuck in and summoned me, calling me to the water's edge. *Come my daughter, dance in my gusts.* I buried my head deeper in my blankets, pretending not to hear. The storm raised in its intensity. *Come now my daughter.* I shook my head, no, I can't, and it's too scary out there. *Come daughter, trust in us.* I tried to stay glued to my cot, pretending it was simply my imagination running away with me. The wind summoning me, yeah, unlikely. As I nestled down and let my heart go back to its usual place in my chest, the cottage door blew open, the fire went out, and the wind was standing above me. *Come right now, daughter, no is no longer a choice.* I rose to my feet, wrapping myself in the blanket and timidly stepped outside of the cottage. It was pitch black. The winds howling, the water crashing. I could feel the spray on my arms and cheeks. I usually am much closer to the shoreline to feel the spray. The water must be nearer than usual. As I continued to step I felt the water rising over my feet. It felt like hundreds of hands grasping at me. I tried to run and pull away.

My screams went unheard, this night. The wind made sure to drown out the sound of my voice. The sea had me and I was being taken. I flailed, screamed, pleaded. "Please no, no, give me back. I do not want to go, please!" My gown now soaking wet, my blanket is gone. I was going out to sea and I didn't know how to swim, not at night, not in a storm. The water over my face and mouth. I couldn't breathe, gasping, reaching towards to the winds to pull me back up.

I could hear music, from far, far away. It didn't comfort me. I was in full struggle, fighting for my breath. Bouncing up with little sips of air between the waves. Praying. Pleading. Wishing to stay alive, this wasn't my time. The sea she didn't know, nor did the wind. I wasn't ready to drown!

Disoriented, tiring, I lay on my back as much as I could and stopped trying to swim. I was getting nowhere, except more tired. I kept bobbing and sinking. Bobbing and sinking. Waves crashing over me—the sea was angry, and I was in her clutches. I felt something brush underneath me. Which given my situation was not surprising, but it did send me a fright. I could feel it coming back again and my pulse quickening in anticipation of its return. Suddenly I was pulled under, at a rapid rate. I could no longer see or feel the winds from the top of the water, I was being taken down into the depths. I held my breath as long as I could....

I woke, inside an underwater cavern. I was breathing. I was breathing! This place was dimly lit and hard to make out where exactly I was, or what was around me. I kept hearing dripping noises and voices in the distance. The music I heard hours before was suddenly right next to me. It was no longer far away, but right here. As though it reached me, or I reached it.

I laid there motionless, afraid to rise. Uncertain of where I was, or what I might find. Maybe I am dead? Or, maybe this is all a dream and I'm actually in my cot sleeping?

My body was heavy with fatigue, moving anywhere quickly wasn't an option. I lay and wait, trying to make out the voices, what they're whispering about. I can hear smacking sounds. Something is slapping in the waters. My curiosity gets the better of me, and I turn to my side, and slowly, ever so slowly begins to open my eyes. Leaving them mostly shut, with a tight squint. I do not want to alert anyone or thing to my waking. I see some type of movement down a few yards from me. Hard to make out the form, exactly. I close my eyes. Listening.

I feel the presence of whatever grabbed me atop the water, approaching me. This presence isn't threatening but is unmistakable. I try not to look for fear of what I may see. It's closer, almost atop of me. I feel it's warmth, this warmth is helping the shivers inside my own body to settle. My mind is racing and I'm enjoying feeling the slightest warmth.

"Welcome. Welcome. We apologize for the way we have greeted you. The storm summoned us, and we weren't quite ready for your arrival."

I began to turn my body over to meet this presence. The voice is calming. The body is warm, how bad can it be? As I make my way over and begin to open my eyes, I am surrounded by an entire colony, troop, swarm, I don't know what it's called; of mermaids and mermen. There must be hundreds of them. The warmth I felt wasn't from one presence, but many.

"Ah, she's awake!" I hear the one closest to me, in her excitement of my waking.

"Where am I?"

"We can't tell you the name, as we know this place as home."

"You are home, but not your home, well, it is your home, welcome home!"

"What do you mean my home? I live on the land in a small stone cottage, near Achill Island. That is my home."

"It was your birthing ground, but this is your home. You are one of us! To be more specific you are a hybrid; half mermaid, half human. You wanted to live amongst them until you were ripening in your womanhood. The sea knew it was time for you to come below and learn about your other qualities."

"My other qualities? This is so strange. Am I dreaming?"

"No, you're not dreaming, you are beginning to wake, wake up to your destiny."

"My destiny? I'm a farm hand, is that not my destiny?"

"No that was your training, not your destiny. You are Yora, a mermaid princess, who was sent to land to help the land dwellers see the beauty of magic and mystery, that encircles them. Your mission is to guide them towards inner compassion, seeing their connection to all things big and small. Encouraging them to become ambassadors of our natural resources. Stop killing mermaids and sea life. We have been waiting for your readiness to welcome you back home. To hear of what you have learned of being human. To begin the waking of all land dwellers!"

"Welcome, Princess Yora!" They all began saying my name and splashing their tails. I lay back down and kept telling myself to wake up. This was all a wild dream, I must have eaten old food, or been given mead. None of this is real.

I woke again to the same mermaid, smiling at me.

"Princess Yora, I'm Biza. I've been watching you from the sea for many moons. We are awakening you to your destiny. You are here to help the world evolve, open their hearts and live in their personal power. Are you not excited?!"

"No, no I'm not excited. I want to go back to my cot and stone walls. I want to pretend none of this is happening."

"You can't pretend to be something you're not. This is why you would stare at the sea for hours upon hours; you knew deep down you belonged here. A part of you remembered where your home lies."

"How am I going to help humanity? Who am I to change anything?"

"Princess, Yora. Do not fret, you have everything you need. You are an integral part of a system. One is no greater or weaker than the whole. All you need to do is allow. Allow your gifts to come out, allow your brilliance to shine. Allow yourself to be fully you. The land dwellers are lost and need our light. We bring ancient wisdom and healing that will evolve those that can't yet see. Those that are lost in their inner darkness. We are the solution, you are the solution. All you need to do is allow."

"What does allowing mean?" I wondered. "How am I to know when I am allowing?"

"Just as the sea grabbed you, you fought. Grasping for the winds to save you. Sipping air, pleading praying. It is no different on the shore. The land dwellers—they too, are sipping and grasping, for something in their life to have meaning, measure. They are drowning, in their shame and guilt. They do not understand that all of this living is a chance to experience the depths of sorrow, togetherness, love. You have learned this from them. With each cobble placed on the foundation for your cottage, a safe haven to dwell, rest from the storms. You have watched them. Felt the human experience. Your immortality cherished cycles, the seasons have endings, and beginnings, everything deepens with the seasons.

"It's now time to trust you, that you've observed these patterns of human behavior and can offer them a beacon, of a safe harbor. You weren't there to save anyone, only understand what pain is. How it feels in the heart. We mermaids do not experience pain, in the same ways that humans do, this is true. As a mermaid, I know that it is all part of the system. That dying is just as natural as living. The only death that comes to mermaids is one created by circumstance from human involvement. It is unfortunate, but it doesn't hurt in the way that human death has affected me. When there is death or tragedy, there is a sense of blame. Remorse for not doing or being more to that person in their lifetime. Mermaids are in the present always, and we do not have regret.

"Humans cling to the idea that tomorrow is a reset. It doesn't excuse the behaviors of today, nor clear the slate. The only way to clear the slate is to deal with the problem. What I can help most with the human condition is learning to express pain. Pain has no place to be held inside the body. When it is there it creates disharmony of the human's internal system. Mood issues, physical pains, anxiety, anger, depression. Pain is meant to be felt and let out. It serves no one to swallow it down and stifle its natural progression. To allow means, letting yourself be seen in your struggle, not fighting the vulnerability. Allowing someone to be there with you. To watch the pain rise and leave, rise and leave. This is allowing."

Do you ever feel that you're destined for something? You can sense something from deep within you wanting to come out. At first a little nudge, or a soft hush that catches your ears attention. As time goes on, this gentle urging begins to grow and before you know it, it's undeniable. Now there is a drive, passion, fire to keep following the crumbs until you reach the end.

That lives within me. It has all of my life. An invisible thread that kept leading me further away from what my life was showing me. I struggle with my own demons, addictions, shortcomings, AND I have a fire within me to change the world. To be known. To be of service. Everything I experienced shaped me, helped me to grow compassion and acceptance at a level I may not have acquired naturally. I was forced to accept things as they were or crumble. To begin living my life instead of drifting on autopilot.

Each and every step was taking me somewhere, giving more fuel to what was once a whisper. I'm now a Clarity Coach, mother of three, wife for almost two decades. Shattering so many of the chains I inherited in my lineage. Helping to heal wounds that haunted our family for decades. Being a mother who learned to be present. To listen and stand in the intensity of my children's pain. Walk in the depths of my own suffering and live with my shadow, learn from it, lead it into the light. I have had an affinity for the shadow my whole life. Everyone I was surrounded by walked in their shadows! It doesn't scare me, I've actually come to find tender appreciation for all that the shadow endures for the sake of its host. In its simplest form, it's a wild dog that has been tied to a post. Unable to roam freely, forage and make its way in the world. It is bound, restless, and hungry for love, acceptance, and care.

When once I wanted to be an actress or nurse, now I am a coach, intuitive medium, energy worker and guide. I help others to walk through their density to discover their brilliance. I would never have thought it possible that I would be able to help another. That my lifetime of learning would be of any benefit, seeing that I am still learning about myself, to better myself, to accept myself. I didn't attend college or do well in school, what I did was pay attention. I learned how to notice people's body language, the space between words, subtle gestures that are told. They give me information that the person may not be ready to see on their own. These little notes that I scribbled in my memory bank, kept me moving forward and alive.

My best certifications are from the school of life. It's an incredible teacher and one doesn't advance until the lesson is complete.

I was staring out the window in sixth-grade English class. My teacher Mrs. Wolfe had the pointiest nose and fingers. She was always shoving one of them in my face to alert me to the fact I wasn't paying attention. Her dull, nasal-sounding language style never piqued my interest. I was far more curious about looking out the window, daydreaming of grand adventures. One day I would be on the Serengeti, another traversing the crusty peaks of Everest. Nothing that was happening in my present-day world captivated me in the same manner as my daydreams. I enjoyed floating in my imagination. Wondering what life would be like outside of the confines of these walls and limits. There was an entire world that revolved around the globes they presented in geography; I found it sad we never visited these places. We never got to explore the terrain in real life. I dreamt often of what the locals would be like. *Did they have a funny way of speaking, would we relate to one another? Would I feel at home in any of these places? Could I outrun a lion? Or would my neck bend far enough back to gaze at a giraffe?* These were the ways I liked to use my brain; to envision a life in the wilds, living amongst the animals, nature. Not being barricaded or locked in anywhere.

I was delighted to find that another woman was already braving the wilderness for her passion: Joy Adamson was living with her lioness, Elsa. She raised her from a cub and they made a movie about her, "Born Free". I remember watching the movie and being captivated by her story. I thought she was a bit odd, choosing a lion after all. They seem more unpredictable than a giraffe or penguin, yet she loved her Elsa, and Elsa may not have known her immense strength. Maybe that is the truest meaning of strength, to reserve it for only survival's sake, and forget about it the rest of the time. That would take great resolve, ignoring your primal nature.

I wondered what animal I would spend the rest of my life observing and caretaking. I knew instantly: a Humpback whale. Though my choice would involve a love for the sea, which I hadn't yet developed. I did, in fact, fall in love with Humpback whales at first sight, thanks to National Geographic magazines, the stiff yellow ones that always had a gorgeous cover on them. When I first saw the whales, I knew that I belonged to them, in some way. I, being a land mammal, would have to find a way to become part of a pod, by vehicle. It seemed possible. "Harold and the Purple Crayon" helped me to imagine the possibilities. I could draw my way through their story. Eventually, they would take notice of my persistence and welcome me as part of the pod. I could swim and play with them, then return to my boat, following along.

When my teacher would smack her ruler or some instrument of sturdy noise making onto her desk, I would pop out of my wild imagination and rejoin the classroom. None of them were as interesting or intriguing as my fantasies.

Maybe God gives us an imagination so we don't forget to have a taste of wonder in the ordinary.

"Opening a Foundation!" I spoke these words as I planned my visioning meeting with Linda (my shadow coach).

We were working on a three-year plan, and what I imagined for my future. My dream, the big one. The one that feels so lofty I can barely keep all of my fingers around it. To open a Foundation dedicated to enlightening people to their shadows in a gentle, playful manner. Removing the weighted stigma that the shadow has come to be known by. I do find it to be like a timid child that has been strung along for too long without rest or refueling. The shadow only needs to know it's safe being known and it softens. The world is ready to know that wholeness isn't through omission, but inclusion. All of the thousands of self-help books covering the aisles—and very few dive into the human shadow. Many tha I've read are dense and difficult to relate to. The late Debbie Ford was th first one to bring levity to something that most psychologists wrote of in clinical sense. Ms. Ford made it tangible for the layman, such as myself, t understand patterning and ill faceted behaviors that I otherwise couldn't describe. Seeing them as my suppressed subconscious behaviors, I began to appreciate how long and hard they have worked to become known.

I feel a plague of our nation is isolation, shame, and detachment from feeling our feelings. The advances in technology have dismantled local community, making it easier than ever to be distracted 24/7. In the past, if a child went missing, the entire community would help look for her. Now she is anonymous within the neighborhood. If a neighbor is ill, the neighbors would know and share the delivery of meals. My next-door neighbor was ill for over a year with cancer and I had no idea. I noticed the signs but ignored my duty to respond because we aren't connected. Shadow behaviors—hiding, believing you're not enough or aren't necessary, are a symptom of a greater problem, the breaking down of social structures in order to gain more control, more power, and isolation. When we aren't connected to one another or our inner light, we make poor decisions and are more bendable to will. This is why coming into direct contact with one's shadow heals the whole. Every time we step into our wholeness we lift the world. It isn't a lofty notion, it is quantum physics.

Letting myself be seen in my shadow and my light has delivered me freedom. Freedom from the worry of what another may think or believe about me. Freedom from what I once found as a flaw within myself. Freedom of expression. Freedom of choice and voice. It returned me to my birthright, Joy. This what I want for the world: Each individual to feel free to be known in their wholeness.

Walking down the tarmac, the blonde in front of me with her yoga pants and running shoes is bouncing. She's looking over her left shoulder to her travel partner with a bright smile. He's looking a little less enthused and fidgets with the strap on his travel bag. With each step, I feel my pulse rising and my cheeks are becoming flush. I am heating up from the inside out, fear racing through me. I've done this a dozen times and even enjoyed myself. Why over the last few years has traveling become a means of great anxiety and distress? The stewardess is wearing the perfect shade of red for her Mediterranean skin. You know how some shades of red look like they were made for the person? Her hair is sparkling to match her lips. The plane is mostly loaded and everyone has a sort of blank stare. The air is hissing from the little holes in the air vents. As we make our way, I am becoming acutely aware of my stress' predecessor. I could pretend that my anxiety stems from the time away from our children. It would be partly true, except that I do enjoy the time away. I used to blame it on the ungrounded feeling I get being 35,000 feet above any visible land. This feeling and its causes are both attributed to something I do have control over, a thing that I can take responsibility for. Instead I'd rather blame and allow my roving anxiety to get the best of me.

We find two seats at the back of the plane. The seats no one would choose because they sit right in front of the bathroom. I'm somewhat comforted by this little nest we have found. As we load our carry-ons, I take the seat in the aisle, Adam the window. Then we fidget and fuss because we have left a seat between us, which means that we would have to hold hands around or with a stranger. We do a shuffle and now I am seated beside the window, he in the middle. We both let out deeps sighs and settle in.

This apparatus they provide to keep one safe—and if it really works I am not sure—is the cause of my massive anxiety. The seat belt is my nemesis. It's my hips' fault; they are robust and aren't meant for flying. My belly would contend that it's definitely the hips, but I know that it's the combination. I am riddled with shame and anxiety and regret of all the choices that have led me here. I am literally centimeters away from no longer being able to fasten the seat belt. My anxiety has been rising for days, in anticipation of this very moment. How humiliating if they ask me to leave the plane, and because of the seat belt that I'm not sure even matters! It may be the reason I can't fly. I keep a low profile and scoot my hoodie over the outside of my belt. If the stewardess asks to see my belt I can show her that it's mostly latched, but if I breathe or cough all bets are off!

I steady my breath through turning my attention back to my inner world. We have come this far, and it's almost time for taking off. I keep telling myself, *"Settle down sweetie, it's all going to be ok."* Adam looks at me and asks if everything is ok. I have forgotten to include him in my mini-drama. I give a reassuring grin and open my left eye. "I'm just centering myself and will be present in a minute or two."

As we leave the ground and begin our ascent, I let out a deep exhale, leaving my anxiety and fears. With my seat belt cutting into me as I take in the view from above, I let my imagination take the reins, giving my body time to relax from the tensions leading up to our travel.

As my mind wanders....

The clouds, like miniature plays, all have their own stories to tell and I let my imagination join them. One cloud bank reminded me of a savannah in the Serengeti. Herds of elephants and giraffes racing past the zebras and gazelles. Later, there were endless mouths filled with cutting teeth looking for anything to gnaw and grind to relieve the pressure.

Nearing our descent, the clouds thickened and neither land nor sea were visible. We were floating in a void, being scanned and checked by the gatekeepers of these lands. The clouds parted and the sea, as blue as ancient glaciers, washed upon the islands that were hidden from our sight by the cloud guardians. I imagine the life of early pioneers, months adrift at sea, no land in sight. Suddenly the clouds part and land-ho! You've arrived at the foothold of forbidden land. The pristine preciousness of God's private playground. Too rich for human footprints.

The pleasure of facing my fears and walking to my seat riddled with anxiety, was being the silent observer to the dramatic set changes in nature's majestic play. The seat belt wasn't an actual hurdle. Allowing my mind to soften around the thoughts about what it would mean if I couldn't participate because of my weight was the obstacle. Something that is a part of me, just as the clouds belong to the sky. I, too, have made amends with my body, a level of appreciation I could only have found at 35,000 feet.

I have had a dysfunctional relationship with my body my entire life. Afraid of being abused for being alluring, I have let the layers pile on top of my frame. Layers of protection and assurance. If anyone still finds me attractive at almost 300 pounds, they must surely be seeing my inner beauty. The truth is, it doesn't matter if they accept me or find me attractive. How I feel matters much more to me at this phase of life. I used to pretend it didn't bother me that I couldn't run or jump. I would pass on having fun because I wasn't sure if I could do the activity, though no one knew that was the reason. I almost missed my 40th birthday surprise party, because I didn't want to be embarrassed if they planned an event that I couldn't handle or would be denied participation in because of a weight restriction. Just as flying created anxiety for me, I have the same anxiety when it comes to anything outside the ordinary routine because of my size. I gave up on trying to help my body when my panic attacks began. I declared war!

It is only a recent interest of mine to understand what my body needs to feel good: What types of foods I should eat, how often I should rest, what types of exercise feel good on my joints. I pay close attention to how I feel as opposed to how I look. Even though I'm not losing weight, I am building trust. Simple activities of walking in my neighborhood create fear for me. I'm afraid my body might give out on me. None of these fears is rational, yet they linger in my cellular memory. One step at a time literally is what I am working with.

Personal acceptance is as layered as love, forgiveness, respect, etc... It all takes time to unwind from the distorted beliefs and create a new way. I no longer need a large frame to protect me. I no longer desire to be unknown or looked over because of my outward appearance. Most importantly, I do not wish to be dismissed or denied because of my weight. I can say it's the other person's problem, but it's not. It's my responsibility to be a healthy weight, a weight that feels good to carry on my frame. To have a physique that I feel strong and confident in. I'm done pretending it doesn't bother me, that my thighs rubbing together is ok. Hiding the fact that I dread the summer because of all the activities, and how uncomfortable it is for me in the heat. Everything sticks and pinches in the summer. I am done with feeling insecure because of the body image I created. I deserve better for myself, and I will create a new appearance.

I used to reward myself with food. Every day at 2:00 P.M. specifically. What did I do every day at 2:00 P.M.? I fed a habit I created to satisfy my need for love and sense of fulfillment, except it never worked. I felt worse afterward nearly every time. I think initially it did feel good until it became a habit. Habits of indulgence don't feel good to me when it comes to food, even if it's greens.

No longer do I fill the house with an excess of food. Now I know that we have more than we need all of the time. This too I am healing. It's another layer on the path to my wholeness. It feels good to admit that I am a food addict. It's the first step to getting better.

Relationships are difficult for me to foster. I have abandonment wounds, trust issues, and perversion around the word love. What does it mean to be loved? How does it feel to receive love? Growing up I would see adults do despicable things to one another and say, "I love you," as if it washed away the wound. I never understood how being harmful meant that you loved the person. It felt like a phrase to hide behind.

My relationship with Faith was highly dysfunctional. Most of my childhood friendships were brief because I didn't live in one place for very long, though somehow Faith kept me in contact with Kelli during all of those moves. I was afraid to be someone's friend. What if we got along well and then I would leave? I didn't know how to cope with leaving or being left. It all felt confusing to me, still does.

Being an empath adds a whole other layer to relationships. I tend to pick up on things that are unspoken. Maybe it's a gesture, a sigh, a head nod, simple things that communicate a lot to me. Learning to be in a relationship with myself seems the most responsible thing to do, and it caused great disharmony in my life. It left those that are/were close to me with feelings of being abandoned. I will admit that I am an abandon-er. I wouldn't have admitted this even a year ago but looking at my history I now see the patterns. I can no longer deny that I have left people without explanation or closure. I ran. Bolted. Fled from their lives, like a criminal at a crime scene. It felt easier this way; any tears I needed to shed could be done solo.

The pitfall? I also abandoned myself. I kept diminishing my own integrity with this behavior, broke trust with myself and others, left myself feeling worse than if I would have just said what needed to be said.

I am sorry

I am sorry for hurting you

Not giving you enough credit

Believing I didn't matter and it would be better for me to leave

Distrusting your ability to handle conflict

Not giving our relationship a chance to deepen

I'm sorry for the missed opportunity to learn

Let my heart be open and unarmored

I am sorry for not believing in you

I am sorry for my ignorance, immaturity

Haste

I am sorry for believing alone was a safe space

I lied to you

I am sorry to anyone who felt harmed by me

Please forgive me.

Chapter Ten
Dribble, Poetry, Miracles

Ways that I have helped myself heal are journaling, therapy, Reiki training, and then becoming a practitioner, teaching Reiki, being an avid student of life gifted with mentors along the path, and mothering. Our children have been instrumental in my own pursuits, because my drive to not screw them up was stronger than my desire to remain stuck in my conditioning. I have always had a love for poetry. Though not formally taught, I do find it helpful in getting my feelings out and processed.

Included here are some of my more poignant pieces along my path. What I lack in "skill" I fill in with being vulnerable. Various cycles in my life brought up different areas of heightened focus. My healing journey has been adventuring in an asteroid belt; some orbits spacious and expansive, others constricted, bumpy and abrasive. Shame is one that has been most predominant in my healing journey. I have organized the poems that capture my processing of my inner churnings and growth.

Many Faces of Shame

Shame, while seemingly well-known to most, has been a mystery to me. It comes in many forms, styles, shapes, and voices. My biggest obstacle with shame wasn't during my shadow walking, it is in capturing my light. The more I embrace my light, the louder the voice of shame becomes. Challenging, and questioning every single step of my expansion. Most notably the inner battle around building a relationship with my intuition and publicly claiming my love for the Divine.

To the chubby girl in the mirror

Let me be clear
The eyes that see you
Are filters of distortion and fear
They're not your reality
They do not see the numerous times you've awakened
Ready to give your all to another day
Anxiously trying new foods
Exercises
Yoga mats
These filters they speak
Words of disgust
Shame
Blame
Disapproval of you
Belittling self-trust
It's not real
They're lies you've been fed
Believed and read
Throughout history
That a waist line
Defines your integrity
Trajectory
Through life
Bullshit!
Has anyone asked
Why?
Why you are bigger than others
What you are holding under the shroud
Of your bulge
It's there to protect
The very thing
That is most delicate
Your heart
Life happened differently for you
That's true
You've dealt with it the best you could
It doesn't define you
It is sculpting
The beautiful creation you are
The charm and wit
Charisma and grit
By which, you lead your agency

You are a force of steel
Graceful as flowing grasses in June
Not to be confused or neglected to ruin
Bestowing Himalayas of compassion
Wild and rampant
You are magnificent
When I look in the mirror and forget what is clear
Smack me
Shake me
Knock me awake
From the distortion
You are a creation of the Beloved
No longer jailed
By my veil or perversion
To be gazed upon
With clarity
Appreciation
For all that you are
All you've overcome
What is next to bloom
You are the beautiful girl in the mirror

"We are not punished for our sins, but by them."

~ Elbert Hubbard

I read this quote in a book by Anne Lamott and it clung like glue. Many times in my life I have done something that was a means of testing limits, mine or someone else's. This was how I learned about life growing up. Often my mistake or sin was looked upon with contempt, scornful eyes, or a finger pointed in my face while being lectured about what a bad child I was.

The punishment still lives inside of me and had me tiptoeing around in my life wondering if I am good enough, acceptable, or lovable. Trying to hide from one more finger being pointed at me, especially my own, because the truth is, my own self-contempt is the most painful.

Now I am learning to parent myself, forgive myself and love the hell out of me. I no longer have to parent my inner child the way I was shown. I can be what I need and ask for help when needed. There is no shame in being me.

You don't get to tell me what to do

What to say
How to act and you certainly will no longer benefit from my shame
I have held onto this heft all of my life
Ashamed to be born
Ashamed to be her daughter
Ashamed of my choices
My shame was always reinforced by everyone else's opinion
You don't make good choices
You're not pretty enough
You're never going to be anything
You weigh too much and would be lucky to have anybody love you
The shame of all of this is that is that I believed it. I believed you, and them.
I am making a stand!
It is ok to make mistakes
It is ok to not know
It is ok to flow in a different direction than the rest
I just didn't fit
I didn't fit the obedient girl corset
Life isn't about being perfect
It's about experience
Learning
Growing
Falling down
Dusting yourself off
Trying again and again
Until you can look at your face in the mirror
Not to fix yourself
To love yourself
To love the mess
The guilt
The shame
The shadow
The light
The victory
The vulnerability
Have compassion for your destiny
It's not linear
It's rough
Bumpy
Some days are hard to raise your head
DO it anyway
You deserve your best

The best moment
The best compliments
Believing in the best you can offer
Love this life
This moment
Love you
It's what makes shame bow down

I sit in my shame

You sit beside me
I wallow in guilt
You wallow beside me
I yell and scream
You rage beside me
You have nowhere to go
You stay loyal beside me
You know this time will pass
You console me
You remind me that good times do last
I rest beside you
You laugh and play
I watch beside you
You are grateful with each new day
I pray beside you
We walk together not the same way
Take solace inside me

You may have done said or felt something
That was not
Kind
Gentle
Or loving towards another
Even yourself
This doesn't mean you are bad
It doesn't mean you should live in shame
It doesn't help your soul to stay bound to
the belief that a moment
reflects a lifetime

You are here to learn
You are trying to expand yourself
It's so damn messy
It can be ugly
It can make you weep

A bad moment(s) doesn't mean you are a bad person!

There is grace in life
It begins with you
Give yourself your own grace
forgive your past
forgive your misdoings
forgive the stunted maturity
that only time helps you to see
You, me, him, her
WE are all trying to learn
Ascend and deepen
Our love of self
So that we can love one another
From a place of pure intent
Not NEED
Not WILL
Not FEAR
Keep forgiving yourself
Letting go
and trust
TRUST that you are
Whole
Beautiful
Worthy

Seasons of Growth

Time chipping away
Each Day
Time chipping away
Pieces of me
What I see is a tiny glimpse
Of a girl I once knew intimately
Time chipping slowly
Steadily
At my masks
Each chip asking is this you?
Does this fit the vision you hold
In the caverns of your heart?
Some days feel like art
Smart
Fresh
Unique
Other's dark
Musty
And I may never breathe again
It's a land of the living and the dead
I hear chants from far off ancestors
Reminding me of why I came
To break through chains of my ancestry
It's my sacred task
One that may not always "look" divine
There are times I live in the dark
Screaming from the walls of my soul
Having nowhere to go
Happening in silence
A quiet sublime rage
Tapping on the cage that surrounds my bones
The sun rises again, I find a ray leaking in
Following it back to the charity of unconditional
Living
It's a lie they tell
To smile
Bow and pretend everything is "fine"
It's a line that I can no longer tow
Breaking chains is arduous
It comes with the price of no longer being nice
But honest
Honest with myself

Honest with the ones I love
Honest with the world
I am here to roar!
Stand back as I claim my birthright
With my bolt cutters in one hand
Roses in the other
Being raw and real
Is the most sacred beauty of all

Today your breath

May move a certain way
Keeping your blood moving
The pain at bay
Today is your day
Be filled with wonder
Not Why, How, or Who
Only worry about you
What you can do
Keep moving
Living
Being your best
Today will be gone
Flow
In the unknowns
Breathe in the now
Knowing
Today is your day
If tomorrow comes
Ease of knowing
You did your best
Lived today feeling
Listening
Opening
To the wonder
Not stuck in plundered regret
Misguided actions
From old patterns
Habits
Impulse
Today is your day
Claim it
Embrace it
It's new
Just for you
Never to repeat
Be your most genuine
To this moment of today

I dread the dark of night

The brightest day
I have suddenly lost my way
My sight, my might.
I once knew who occupied the space from my
Toes to my face
Now she's a stranger.
I lost her in this relationship
Of necessity and false praise
In the haze of my wanting to
Be loved, connected
I will go inside, rummage through the rubble
Of what was once a foundation.
I have faith, trust, and purpose.
The clarity will come
For now, I sit with the horror of the unknown
Feeling safer here than many days
In what was familiar.

Give yourself some credit
Yes
You!
You may not be where you want to be
You are where you're choosing to be
There is no foul in the game of life
Except
For the sidelines
If you're there, know you can move
If you don't want to
That's cool
Stop complaining or
Comparing
You've made the choice
If you're busting ass
Pause
Take in the sights
The joy is in the space in between
Applaud yourself
Your passion
Your vision
Are driving your chi
Every single second we have here
Is propelled by our choice
If you don't like the place you're in
Choose new
Choose to stretch
Choose the uncomfortable
Choose
You!
Every time
You can't go wrong

Birthing of the Warrior Many times along the way I have been bestowed with compliments of my courage, strength, and bravery. The irony is I never saw these qualities in myself. I saw a girl trying to be a woman, in a land of fog and distortion. I didn't know what bravery looked like. I wasn't sure if courage meant facing the demons or running. Both seemed appropriate at times. What I carry in my heart now is the knowing that it's a messy excavation. With no set path, or right turns to make along the way. My strength can now only be defined as my will to keep circling up the spiral. I may fall, trip even slide back down a few floors, but now I know with certainty I will get up and try again. This is my superpower. I call her Destiny.

I know a girl

Maybe you do too
That is sensitive to this world
Cries four times a day
Trying to flush away
The energy
People
Actions
Events
That oppress
And circumvent
Her joy
They don't know that's what they've done
Moving mindlessly
And on the run
She sees it feels it
It clings to her cells
So confused and weighed down
By the hells of society
On a day she may not recall
She said fuck it all
And got mad
She started saying no
And go away
Making every minute in her life
Adhere to the way
She wanted to breathe
Feel and live
It wasn't selfish
Bitchy
Rude
It was her survival
Food
It had to be

Not one more minute or tear
Could hide her fear
She had to face it
With her voice
Choice
Swagger
Sway

That was the only way
Stoking the heat
From deep beneath
Her tears
Giving sparks
Igniting
The Wild Woman
Cheers
Burning away
The fears
Birthing the
Flames!

There's a voice growling
From inside her chest
Tired of pretending
Playing
A game of how to impress
She was bred to satisfy
The whims and needs
Of others
She's had enough
Broken heart
From the very start
Life of dismay
Gasping for air
No one showed care
Did they know she was there?
She's had enough
A pawn in another's game
Walking, running away
Wasn't enough
She pleads to be supported
Her own needs more important
Create a new way
She's had enough
Time to satisfy her hearts
Longing
Pulling out the arrows of other's wronging
It's a new start
Writing a new story
She rises in her glory
Burning all that kept her bound
To a false expectation
Not of her own ground
She is enough

As tears flood my eyes

Dance down my face
It's no surprise why they're here
The echoes of fear
Hanging from my heart
Pulling back another layer
Goodbye
Shame
Regret
Humility
Abandonment
Places I hide
Squandering my brilliance
My inheritance
To be all of me
Not to be pigeonholed by mistakes
Blundered
Moments of confusion
Leading to self-abuse
Harsh voices
Hiding
Damming
Pushing away
Anything that gets too close
To my illusion
Of being unworthy
Unsavory
Lowly
I'm fatigued
From denying
My divinity
My shine
My nobility
That's right
Nobility

I dry my eyes
Adjust my belt
Dive back in the rhythm of life
Flow in the knowing
Of where I'm going
Not from a voice of confusion
A choice
My choice to live a life of transcendence
Not obedience

I stand my face to the sun

The quiet revolution of my heart has begun
You stand on the shore
Patient loving supportive
Ready and steady
Seeing the power of self-support
Allowing me to stand tall
No expectations or walls
Ready
My heart knew the first time, it was you
Ready
Years of conditioning, fear, pain
Washing away day by day
I am ready
No more living a life of maybe or mediocrity
As a rouse of safety
I am ready
To embrace the life god has for me
Love
Truth
Divinity
I am ready
Come with me....

The war of not knowing

Unlike a soldier who readies himself for battle
I was the army, the cause, the recruiter, strategist, no one the victor
Growing up with tangible shadows as my caregivers
I unknowingly sent myself to battle
Years of fighting enemy lines against unworthiness, self-hate, distrust, loathing
Forty years of proving, forcing, struggling
To find a sense of freedom
Certitude
Authenticity
The pain at times unbearable
The tension of what was
What is not yet to be
Stayed numb to breathe
To swim in casks of beer
Clouds of smoke
Mind and ego
Awakening to a whole new habitat
Relearning to feed, walk, live
in an unfamiliar location
Trusting that the community of air
Will breed similarity and camaraderie
Spiraling inward to see
The hidden parts of me
No more perfume to cover
The stench of deception
I go alone
No room for two
With fervor
And a chisel
I descend
Into the mystery of the sea
Emotions
Notions
Reverie

My Shadow

I have an affinity for the human shadow. It's a simple and complex system; when handled with care, excavates the fullest expression of one's soul. The shadow spends most of its existence hidden and unknown. To dismiss this part of oneself is more harmful than helpful. Making peace with my shadows is what has set my past free. I spent many years diving deep, walking alone and learning. My shadow has taught me much about my complexity, fears, strengths and gifts. It was in the depths I found my creative expression, right underneath the sorrow.

The beauty of my shadow

Can't always be seen
Sometimes
Harsh
Withdrawn
Mean
She lives in every cell of my being
Loving me
Holding me
Helping me to see
Can you hear me
Do you feel my will
It's time we took a walk over the hill
The hill of fear, avoidance and shame
You have no one to blame
This is your game
Will you be with me?
Love me
Open to me?
Will you trust this is good for both of us
The ones who fear you
Fear me
They only see a part of me
The more raw
Unrefined
Untamed parts of yourself
Do not worry
Or rush
Integration is a process
Resulting in wholeness

What do you see when you look in the mirror? Mirrors are people, glass, chrome, reflections, water, etc. Mirrors are everywhere in our life. What do you see when you allow yourself to really look at what is being shown?

I could say my hair is wild and frizzy.

The puffiness under my eyes is growing.
My summer kissed glow is fading.
The scar above my nose bugs me.
Or
I can look deeper into my own eyes.
See what my soul is trying to help me realize.
I am so much bigger than this costume I wear each day.
The me I see is not, the me I am
I have a wild rhythm that is growing.
It has a primal beat, not of this existence.
It is the countless versions of me that worked to bring me to this now moment.
And
It is through the mirrors of people, I am shedding outdated beliefs.
I am letting go of the expectations of how I am supposed to be, who I am supposed to be, what I am supposed to be.
The mirrors of inanimate objects are helping me to catch glimpses of my undomesticated self.
To get to the purer form of this primal beat.
Allowing it to lead my heart into the unknown.
Face my fears.
Scream when I need.
Fall to my knees in humility, that I do not KNOW anything when it comes to living from this place. If I allow the voices of this world and this race.
I am too far in to retreat. Too curious to stop. I keep looking in the mirrors, with my palms face up. I am willing to receive the untamed version of me.

Too hungry to eat

Too restless to sleep

Like an animal scratching at the door
Desperate for shelter before the storm

Howling on the winds
Are my soul's wishes
Not whimsy
Refusing to be ignored
Dishonored
Or abhorred
She Howls
Enticing me to gaze into the eyes of her storm
To bow down in surrender
That what is coming to be
Will be my normal

No longer accepting excuses
I'm too tender
I feel weak
Too afraid to speak

Rise she howls
Stand on your feet
Dig in deep if you must
There will be times you will weep
Release the need to be humble
Or hide

There's a fire burning deep
The flames continue to rise
Your time is coming
Listened to the drumming of your restless heart
Open your eyes to the reality
You are your own prize

It's not a lover
Fame or fortune you seek
It's your own essence
The presence of you and your alone
That drives your calling
To see the marrow in your bones

Open to your power
Your magic
There's nothing in front or behind you
Your confusion, hunger and thirst
Are illusions
Come now child
Open your breasts
Surrender to your divinity
Shadows

Nighttime shadows
Monsters behind the shed, under my bed or, maybe in my head
Are they big, scary, mean
Just tired of not being seen by the lady instead
Shadows absorb the light
They do not frighten the curious
Delight in the mystery of space between the known and unseen

A poem for my children

These tears I shed
I shed for us
The air of the reality
Is but dust
Of a time when
I was the age of you
I didn't know what to do
I had bouts of blue
Fear and disgust
I blow away this dust
Trusting that this day we share
Not be clouded in fear
I know what to do
I listen
To the person you are
Not the memory or scar
That I once held in my heart
We have a new day a new start
I listen
I step into this day with an open heart
For you get to be you
Without the memory of me clouding the moment
I listen
Present, open, breathing
And so begins the healing on this new day
I wipe my tears
Embrace the chance to stand here with you
I listen

Love

It's not something you can be shown
It's something you need to learn
If we were told we would not believe
It's our job to upheave
The truths of our souls yearning
Feel the burning
Of walking in a new way
Breathing in the magnificence
Of this new way
Life

The day I learned to love myself was an ordinary day; the girl in the mirror looked the same way

The way I saw her was new

The way I felt about her was new

I no longer looked at her to criticize

I stared deep into her eyes and for the first time, said, "I love you." Wherever we go from here, it will always be me and you

I am here to take good care of you

Tears of Humanity

I'm the tear tree
Holding the tears of humanity
Sadness
Happiness
Uncertainty
Fright
All flowing through the depth of my roots
To the heights of my canopy
Please do not feel sorry for me
I am humbled by my duty
Divine sovereignty
It is I that rains down on cloudy days
Keeps misting the mornings of the San Francisco Bay
Why one might say
To keep harmony
Of tender hearts
Puddling eyes
Peoples filled with surprise
All the tears come through me
Back to soak the cheeks
Of anyone who chooses
To release the tears of humanity

Love is not always bouquets, cards, and butterflies, easy
There's a deeper more brick and mortar place from love
Tissues, hard conversations, messily painful squirmy kind of love
The love that's too embarrassing to receive because, why would someone like me with all of my faults, be lovable
Letting love find you, when you're hiding is hard. It's uncomfortable.
It's real
Real love isn't judging you
Denigrating you
Damming you to be something you're not
Love finds your inner fissures, distortions, and touchy spots
Then ever so gently and steadily says, "I'm here, I'll wait until you're ready to let me in."
I love you, the whole you

Loving a warrior
Isn't about words actions or doings
It is the way that you walk in the world
The way you held your pain and saw it through to the end
Knowing that inside of your chest beats a tender heart that no longer fears what may, or may not be

You are comfortable with uncertainty, living for the presence of each moment, experience
Taste
Delight
Fulfillment
You know yourself well
You are curious to learn more
That is when you can extend your hand to the warrior
She too has walked that road
She is not looking for someone to save her she saved herself
She will welcome you
If you can stand tall
In all of her Fury
Then you may open your arms
Carry her through the rest of Eternity
From the battlefield of love

Miracles

After meeting The Big Quiet and beginning my healing journey, I had countless experiences that are somewhat jumbled, as I paid closer to attention to the experiences than the order with which they happened.

Lori was teaching a class on the four clairs; hearing, seeing, feeling, and knowing. As I listened to her describe the feeling sense known as Clairsentient, I had a sense of relief as most of what I was experiencing was coming from the energies around me, not from me. I was perceiving more than myself! EUREKA!

I didn't know what being empathic was, or that there was a name for some of the experiences I had encountered throughout my life. I had psychic abilities that were underdeveloped.

I came to the ancient healing art of Reiki. My Reiki teacher, Sue Ball, spent many hours with me helping me to curate my intuitive experiences, to keep looking into the unknown with curiosity not fear. It was through my Reiki training and reconnection to my suppressed self that I began developing my intuition, which led me to exceptional mentors along the way; Rian, Lori, Debi, Sue, Melinda, Deborah King, HeatherAsh Amara— just to name a few.

What began with number sequences 11:11, 333, 12:34, morphed into license plates, and then voice-ish—not a disembodied, unknown or scary voice—more of a narrator that shared things I would never know about a person. Slowly things began to make more sense to me about the way I sensed energy in the world (clairsentient) my panic disorder (overwhelmed parasympathetic system).

I am a medium. This wasn't a revelation that happened in one instance but a series of succession that led me to the awareness that I am able to perceive, receive, and deliver messages from those on another plane of existence. Some call them deceased; others may say angels, guides, ancestors. I can also relay messages at times from those still living. However one defines it, I called it miraculous attunement. It's not a gift, but practice of growing my own awareness, along with my energy body to set the station to receiving. I would not take back one ounce of my journey for where it has brought me is seeing and experiencing things that brought me to a place of service. Being of service fills my heart and allows my spirit to breathe.

While driving, Michael and I were having a conversation about purpose. I was speaking with him about how I experience the intense power of purpose and how it feels like 5000 watts of raw energy squeezing through a 200-watt outlet. It can be so squeezy and painful that I don't know what to do, BUT I can't ignore it. If I ignore it, it keeps calling and ringing my line. I can choose to say; "No thank you, you have the wrong number." And, it will keep checking back in.

He said, "What do you do? How do you help the purpose, when it feels stupid to anyone else or a bad time?"

I said, "You keep your faith higher than your fears. You put all your trust in the purpose and know it will lead you. That flow of energy will take you where you need to be to serve, when you need to be there and how you show up."

By this time tears are pouring down my face. I know he is my messenger. I know he is inviting me to listen to my own truth be spoken. He knows I am afraid right now. That I am reorienting my life AGAIN in order to keep the line open for my purpose.

In my periphery, I saw this white car deciding if it would pull in front of us or not. Sure enough, it darted out and I immediately took note of the license plate, "1 ROXIE."

My mother wanted to name me Roxanne. In that very moment, I could feel her wrap me in a spirited hug. And the tears now transferred to our son as well. I said, "Look, honey, Grandma Red is with us. She is supporting us and giving hugs!"

The whole ride was my reminder: To keep moving forward. Keep believing in myself. Keep my faith high and my devotion to the forefront. Purpose doesn't always mean changing the whole world. My purpose can be as subtle as changing my own world, which heals the lineage I am a part of.

On another day, when I was driving alone, I was repeating the Hoʻoponopono prayer to Faith. If you're unfamiliar it goes:

I love you

I am sorry

Please forgive me

Thank you

She passed almost 11 years ago, and I am still healing from who I was in our relationship. Also, the grudges I held because I didn't understand why she was who she was. Immediately following, I turned on the radio and heard Sting belt out Roxanne.

Another clear sign from Faith. She would joke with me that she chose Brigid Moran instead of Roxanne because she felt I'd have more political pull later in life. Thankfully I was named after my fiery, spunky, great, great grandmother who was Brigid Moran.

It felt great having the confirmation, and a chuckle, that my mother is never far away.

I have been healing wounds regarding my departed grandmother. Though she passed when I was young, I never dealt with the impact!

Her formal name was Geraldine, even though she was nicknamed "Bobo." Why Bobo, I'm not sure.

As I continue to heal and integrate, I have been asking for her support and to gently guide me.

I say, "Please be with me, and let your sign be clear and unmistakable."

This car was in front of me yesterday. I'd say she nailed it! It helps to soothe my wound, knowing that only a veil of perception separates us.

Building relationships isn't only for the living. I have a better relationship and appreciation for my mother eleven years after her passing.

And while I never really knew my Dad in the physical, opening to my intuition gifted me with receiving his love, guidance, and support!

I'm coming out of my emotional closet. I'm letting myself be known as an empath.

For years I have overcompensated by being an extrovert; over confident, overly assured, and seemingly impenetrable. Too afraid my heart would be crushed, or taken advantage of if anyone knew how sensitive I am.

Life has a way of unweaving the web of self-deception.

I am an introvert
I am sensitive
I feel everything
I perceive more than people realize
I need time to recharge
Big crowds are overwhelming
I can sniff untruths spoken or not
I am vulnerable
I ache for our world

And—

I am in charge
I offer what I can from a full cup
I take care of my needs
I keep learning how to stay open and empathic
I trust my intuition
I have boundaries
I no longer over-give
I no longer push away from things that scare me
My closet is open, I'm unashamed. I'm allowing myself to be known as I am.

Chapter Eleven
It's Hard to Say Goodbye

As we glide through the city streets, the streetlights are reflecting on the rinsed ground, the air clingy to my curls. Everything looks clean and renewed; though peering out the window isn't as entertaining as watching Faith.

Her bright red hair refracts the light, which illuminates the interior of her 1974 Gremlin. The interior is sticky and smells like an old musty attic. I do not like that I stick to the seats.

"Mom, why are the seats so sticky?"

"Because it's raining baby, I think it does something to the vinyl."

I am certain the vinyl material was made to torture the riders! She is humming to a song on the radio; her eyes are twinkling, head bobbing in rhythm. Her hand on the wheel, with an ash hanging off her Winston cigarette. I marvel at how long the ash could grow before falling.

"Downshift!" she hollers.

Feeling startled, I mumble, "What?"

"Downshift, now!"

I quickly grab the gear shift. I have been her assistant driving a manual car for two years now, as she only has use of her left arm, the same arm holding her cigarette.

She glances over at me with a glassy eyed smile. "Thanks, baby." The twinkle is more of a stoned glassy glare head on. I smile back. This is how it is with Faith. She pops a pill and lives in a hazy moment of her reality. It leaves me on edge and paying attention is important. She moves fast, lives hard, and is always looking to find any excitement in the ordinary.

Sitting at the light, she reaches over and reaches for a tape in the glove box. She's fumbling through the papers and miscellaneous clutter.

"Ah, there it is."

"Please don't, I can't stand that album."

"Ok, ok," she says with a hushing, soothing tone. "I'll only play one song, promise."

"Are you planning to play The Song?"

"Do you mind?"

"Yes, I mind, it grates my nerves." We begin moving, I'm shifting the stick.

"Come on Brigid, let's do it for old time's sake.

"It's not my old time, it's yours and it feels torturous!"

"Just once, please. Pretty please…"

"Fine!" I let out a deep sigh. Away we go with Johnny Cash belting out, "I walk the line," Faith smiling at me. I stare out the window and let her have her moment. Faith and Johnny, I'm only along for the ride. The third arm…

Acknowledgements

This book would never have existed if it weren't for the unusual turn of events at Faith's funeral. It was on that day that Adam and Nichol egged me on to write this book. Though it took me close to twelve years to bring it forward, I am forever thankful for all of the minutes and experiences that gave breath to this project.

Adam you were and are tirelessly patient with me! We have walked through the fires of life, always emerging on the other side, tempered, and not hardened. You have given me the chance to leave survival mode and turn towards thriving. <3

My mother, Faith. Honoring the woman who was my first trainer, I am a warrior; not because I wear armor and fight to the death. I am a warrior who stands on the front line of her own inner demons with the eyes of understanding, curiosity, care, and warmth. Faith's legacy lives in me and grows in my children. She is why I am here; the pain between us is now the humus in my garden. Each word, chapter, and tear shed while reviewing our story was beautifully difficult. What I couldn't give in her life, I am trying to correct in my life for her grandchildren. Together we rise.

To our children Alex, Mae, and Michael. You are the reason I am eager to wake to a new day. You're the dawn in my heart, even when the lights are out. You always give me the chance to let love in..

Nichol G., who knew my strength before me. It took me time to see it for myself. You always believe in me. Who could ask for more?

Jillian my early awakener to being validated, seen and loved. You said yes to the unknown and it sure has been fun!

My patient, honest keeper of my words, Beth Rowles. All the time you gave to editing a book that had little grammatical correctness, but a lot of heart! You kept the essence of my voice intact. Thank you!

Aunt Mary and Sharon who carefully tend all of our family's history. Aunt Mary showed me how to care for the headstones of our relatives when I was a young girl. It is something I am teaching our children how to do, because remembering those who walked before us is sacred.

All of the early whisperers encouraging me to give writing a go, and or, to keep sharing my insights with others. -- Trish, Jenny D., Jen G., Sarah B., Alecia P., Rani, Gillian K., Rian Dean, Amy P., Tony G., Julia M., Linda Yeazel, Turmalin Spirit, Lori C., Jimmye L., Lylia S., Mindy S., Meagan C., Samantha S., Tiffany Savion, Manpreet, Nimita, Erin Taylor, Cara Pollard, Sue DeCaro, Michelle Jacobs, Patricia Barros, Tammy W, Sandra Fazio., Georgia Petersen DeClark—your encouragement never went unnoticed, it simply took me time to receive it. My heart thanks you for lifting me above my limited perspective!

My Sacred Pod--We have shed many skins, always evolving and deepening our roots!

All of my sisters from Woman Within, what happens in circle, stays in circle! You have held my eruptive growth with the grace of angels.

Sister Gardeners at the Lake Erie Institute— your care and nurture are my home away from home. <3

My writing guide Jack Ricchiuto—your patience helped me to bloom, in a place I didn't know I'd been planted.

ALL of my clients, your courage inspires my own.

My Warrior Goddess Sisters—showing up for ourselves each day, facing down the dragons and releasing more of our divine grace.

Friends and fellow writers of the Lit Cleveland Memoir group: you've helped me to stay courageous when I most needed it--shaking voice, tearful eyes; you never looked away and always gave sincere feedback.

HeatherAsh Amara, you were the container for the unfurling of this young sprout. Your ancient wisdom, graceful nurture, and warrior courage showed me my inner sparkle. I'm forever grateful.

The Ford Institute for guiding me and countless other's back to their light.

One may think the most difficulty I faced when writing this book was peering through the foggy windows of my youth to extract some type of clarity to help myself move on. The most difficulty was in fact sitting down each day to write. I had major resistance to this project. Every day I would tell myself some variation of; what a waste of time it is to write this book, who cares, I'm not even that interesting, I'm a terrible writer... you get the idea. Yet, here I am on the final page. Thank you for walking through my history with me. May we meet in the sunlight of lives explored, measured and seasoned, with a bit more compassion toward the past and excitement for the future.

Until then....